Training Sessions For Soccer Coaches Volume 3

Training Sessions For Soccer Coaches, Volume 3

Chris King

Published by Chris King, 2023.

TRAINING SESSIONS FOR SOCCER COACHES VOLUME 3

First edition. August 31, 2023.

ISBN: 979-8223278139

Written by Chris King.

TRAINING SESSIONS FOR
SOCCER
COACHES
VOLUME 3
Coaching Books For Amateur Soccer Coaches
CHRIS KING
THE KING SOCCER COACH

TRAINING SESSIONS FOR SOCCER COACHES - VOLUME 3

by Chris King

INTRODUCTION

This book is for amateur, grassroots soccer coaches who want to improve their training sessions (and in turn their match day performance from their team).

"Training Sessions for Soccer Coaches - Volume 3" lays out full training sessions that will improve different parts of your team's game. **It walks you through what to do from the warm up to the warm down and all the drills in between.**

The drills in this book are explained step by step and include diagrams. They will have you running a quality training session in no time.

These training sessions have been chosen because they work in real life, not just in a book. I run all these sessions with my team. These drills will bring improvement to you and your team.

These drills are 100% on the ball so they improve endurance, technique, and tactics all at the same time plus you'll see your players enjoying the sessions more.

If you're a new coach, volunteer, parent or you're simply a coach that hasn't had the time **to work on your sessions, this book will improve you immensely. Game day results start on the training track and if the coach doesn't have a good training session planned, the players won't improve and will lose motivation.**

Most drills can be adjusted to suit the number of players you have at your session. I understand that on any night player numbers vary, so most of these drills are adjustable for more or less players.

I've completed coaching courses and coached senior men's teams, ladies, youth and children's teams, so I have a well rounded knowledge of different teams and different standards.

The advice and drills in this book will get you up and running straight away. Don't jump on YouTube an hour before training looking for a fancy drill - **simply choose a session from this book, follow the step by step guides and you will see your sessions and coaching ability improve straight away** (plus you'll enjoy coaching more!).

The drills focus on one main aspect per session and you are given three different drills per session that build on each other. you will learn how to run drills for key components of the game such as:

1. **Playing Out From The Back**
2. **Switching The Play**
3. **Defending 1v1**
4. **Attacking Corners**
5. **Goalkeeper Essential Skills plus much more**

The drills are all aimed at improving players technical ability and all of the drills are 'on the ball'. I believe in getting fit and improving skill through football based drills, not just running for the sake of running. As a coach, you may only have the players for two 90 minute sessions a week, so the training sessions laid out in this book help you get maximum value out of those sessions.

Before you jump into the first session, please spend 5 minutes reading the following chapter which breaks down how a general training session should be structured.

Online Kids Coaching Course on Udemy.com: **https://www.udemy.com/course/howtocoachkidssoccer/?referralCode=CCFEDDB18FE0AAF8F1CC**

TRAINING SESSION STRUCTURE

A training session with a non-professional senior team should run for approximately 90 minutes (*__not__* including initial warm up or warm down).

Using a topic or theme for the night (ie Playing Out From The Back) helps to get "buy-in" from the players. They can see there is a focus for the training session and that the coach has put thought and planning into what they will be doing.

Let's break it down into an average 90 minute Tuesday night training session at my club.

I realise some coaches may only have an hour or so with their teams so if that is the case, you may want to cut 5 minutes off each of numbers 1,4,5,6 and 7 and if possible, encourage them to get there earlier and do their own light warm up.

Listed below is how I run my session so you can get an idea:

(Please note, in Volume 1 and 2 of Training Sessions For Soccer Coaches it is a slightly different format with 4 main parts to the sessions. This book will focus on having 3 main parts to the session - Drill A,B and C).

1. **6:00 - 6:10: Players Getting Ready To Start (Light Warm Up)**

1. **6:10 - 6:15: Training Starts: Coach Short Introduction Talk**

1. **6:15 - 6:35: Warm Up (the FIFA 11+[1])**

1. **6:35 - 6:55: Drill A (The Learning Phase [usually a Rondo drill])**

1. **7:00 - 7:25: Drill B (The Development Phase)**

1. **7:30 - 8:05: Drill C (The Game Phase)**

1. **8:05 - 8:15: Warm Down**

Numbers 4,5 and 6 (Drills A,B and C) are the drills that change from session to session and are all covered in detail in this book.

1. PLAYERS GETTING READY TO START (Light Warm Up):

The players should have their training gear on and do individual light warm ups (foam roller, band stretching, etc) while talking to each other, interacting and having a laugh for 10 minutes.

---

1. https://www.youtube.com/watch?v=RSJIp7e7fyY

This part should not be underrated! It gives the players a chance to catch up and bond. Plus it will make them more focussed later on as they will have already had a chat and a laugh so they can focus more on the session.

2. TRAINING STARTS: COACHES SHORT INTRODUCTION TALK:

A short 5 minute talk by the coach (you!) on the areas that will be covered in tonight's session (this helps you get player 'buy in' for the session. Players start to understand they're here to learn and work hard, alongside fitness and having fun).

3. WARM UP:

The Warm Up should be the FIFA[2] 11+[3] every time. It has been proven to reduce injuries and players can chat and bond at the same time. *This should run for approximately 15-20 minutes.*

(Note: Most parts of the FIFA 11+ should be performed before a match as well)

4. Drill A (The Learning Phase) Note: Usually a Rondo drill

Next is always Drill A, which is The Learning Phase. It is usually a Rondo which is a simple short, sharp drill in a small area. It gets the players body and mind warmed up for the session and introduces the skill or part of the game that will be worked on for the session. *This should run for approximately 15-20 minutes.*

5. Drill B (The Development Phase)

Drill B is The Development Phase. It is a progression from Drill A and is used to get the players thinking about where they should be on the pitch and what role they should play. The drill is usually in a small to medium sized area so players get lots of chances to repeat the parts that are being worked on. *This should run for approximately 20-25 minutes.*

6. Drill C (The Game Phase)

It's time for a game (11v11, 5v5, whatever numbers you have).

At the end of the night you should always have a game. It's great to do drills but eventually it has to be implemented in a match situation, so this is when you do it. There shouldn't be many (if any) restrictions. Let your players play and hopefully they implement what you have been working on in the session.

2. https://www.youtube.com/watch?v=RSJIp7e7fyY

3. https://www.youtube.com/watch?v=RSJIp7e7fyY

Look for key moments from the session that night that you have been working on that appear during the game.

Then stop the game briefly to point out what they are doing correctly or incorrectly. But generally just let the game flow and observe your players. *This should run for approximately 30-35 minutes.*

8. WARM DOWN:

The warm down should be 10 minutes of light jogging, walking and intermittent static stretching.

That's a general overview of what a training session should look like.

Please Note: There's an index at the back of the book for a few terms that will pop up that you may not be familiar with. Plus the FIFA 11+ Warm Up is covered towards the end of the book.

PLAYER NUMBERS FOR THE SESSION

Most of the sessions in this book are adjustable for different amounts of players.

As a coach I realise that on most occasions you may not know exactly what numbers you will have for a particular session. Sometimes players pull out before the session due to work or personal reasons or they get injured during the session.

As a coach you have to be adaptable. So please keep the following two main tips in mind when running sessions and it will help you adjust on the fly:

1. **Use A Joker**

A "Joker" is simply an extra player that usually plays for both teams (i.e. plays on the team in possession).

So if you have an extra player (or you want to overload the attacking or defending team) add in a Joker.

For example, you may be playing a possession based game with 5 players on the red team and 5 on the green team but you have 11 players. Add in a Joker in a Blue top and they play with the team who has the ball.

I find using a midfielder as the Joker works well as they get to practice lots of passes. Plus they have to have awareness and speed of thought of what is happening around them.

1. **Set Up A Mirror Of The Drill**

This simply means set up an extra copy of the drill you are about to run in case you have too many players and need to split up.

I know this won't be practical for full ground sessions or if your space is limited. But if you're running a smaller drill and you have the space, it usually won't take much effort to set up a mirror image of the drill next to it.

It's easier to remove a few cones if you don't need them instead of having to add more and keep the players waiting!

And even if it's a large drill, can you set up another station in case you have too many players and then some can move to this extra station?

For example, if it's a shooting drill and you have 2 strikers on 2 stations, 2 wingers on 2 stations and the rest near the halfway line on a station - can you add in another station in front of the halfway line stations so that players can do a bounce pass to start the drill and therefore 2 players can move to that station and players aren't waiting. **We don't want long lines or players not involved! All players should be getting as many touches as possible in every training session).**

That's enough for now, I'm sure you want to start looking through the first drills, so read on and use my session plans and watch your coaching improve.

VIEW OTHER SOCCER COACHING BOOKS BY CHRIS KING

Training Sessions For Soccer Coaches Volume 1

Training Sessions For Soccer Coaches Volume 2

Training Sessions For Soccer Coaches Volume 3

Attacking & Shooting Drills For Soccer Coaches

Soccer Rondos Volume 1

Soccer Rondos Volume 2

Coaching Kids Soccer - Volume 1

Coaching Kids Soccer - Volume 2

Coaching Kids Soccer - Volume 3

The Ultimate Soccer Coaching Bundle Volume 1

110 Drills For Soccer Coaches

TRAINING SESSIONS FOR
SOCCER
COACHES
VOLUME 1
Coaching Books For Amateur Soccer Coaches
CHRIS KING
TRAINING SESSIONS FOR 
SOCCER
COACHES
VOLUME 2
Coaching Books For Amateur Soccer Coaches
CHRIS KING
TRAINING SESSIONS FOR
SOCCER
COACHES
VOLUME 3
Coaching Books For Amateur Soccer Coaches
CHRIS KING
TRAINING SESSIONS FOR
2 BOOKS IN 1
SOCCER
COACHES
VOLUMES 1+2
Coaching Books For Amateur Soccer Coaches
CHRIS KING

TRAINING SESSIONS FOR
SOCCER
COACHES
3 BOOKS IN 1!
VOLUMES 1,2,3
Coaching Books For Amateur Soccer Coaches
CHRIS KING
ATTACKING & SHOOTING DRILLS FOR
SOCCER
COACHES
VOLUME 1
Coaching Books For Amateur Soccer Coaches
CHRIS KING

SOCCER
RONDOS
VOLUME 1
Coaching Books For Amateur Soccer Coaches
CHRIS KING
SOCCER
RONDOS
VOLUME 2
Coaching Books For Amateur Soccer Coaches
CHRIS KING

2 BOOKS
IN 1
SOCCER
RONDOS
VOLUMES 1+2
Coaching Books For Amateur Soccer Coaches
CHRIS KING

COACHING KIDS SOCCER
AGES 5 TO 10
VOLUME 1
This book is for first time coaches, volunteers, parents and anyone wanting to coach!
Set up simple, fun and effective drills and organise a training session in 5 minutes!
CHRIS KING
COACHING KIDS SOCCER
AGES 5 TO 10
VOLUME 2
This book is for first time coaches, grassroots coaches, volunteers and parents!
Set up simple soccer drills that teach kids skills while having fun!
CHRIS KING

COACHING KIDS SOCCER
AGES 5 TO 10
VOLUME 3
This book is for first time coaches, volunteers & any would be coach
Set up simple, fun and effective drills & organise a practice session in 5 minutes!
CHRIS KING
2 BOOKS IN 1
COACHING KIDS SOCCER
VOLUMES 1-2
This book is for first time coaches, volunteers & any would be coach
Set up simple, fun and effective drills & organise a practice session in 5 minutes!
CHRIS KING

COACHING
KIDS SOCCER
VOLUMES 1,2,3
This book is for first time coaches, grassroots coaches, volunteers and parents!
Set up simple soccer drills that teach kids skills while having fun! Includes 3 Volumes!
CHRIS KING

THE ULTIMATE
SOCCER
COACHING
BUNDLE
VOLUME ONE
5 BOOKS IN 1!
CHRIS KING
110
DRILLS FOR
SOCCER
COACHES
7 BOOKS IN 1!
Coaching Books For Amateur Soccer Coaches
THIS BOOK INCLUDES 7 BOOKS IN 1!
CHRIS KING

KING
SOCCER
COACH

— FULL TRAINING SESSIONS

—

SESSION 1: POSSESSION UNDER PRESSURE

Session Objective:

Improving players' ball retention under pressure.

SESSION 1 "POSSESSION UNDER PRESSURE"
DRILL A (THE LEARNING PHASE)
"4v2 PRESSURE"

� PURPOSE:

- Keeping possession and composure under pressure.
- Good quality passing under pressure.
- Creating space.
- Defenders learn to hunt the ball and put extreme pressure on the opposition.

� SET UP:

- **12 Players (Alternatively 9 to 16 Players**. Have 4 Attackers in the middle and the rest as Defenders waiting to come in).
- 10x10 yard square

� THE DRILL:

In this setup there are 12 players.

4 players (Attackers) start inside the square. The remaining 8 players (Defenders) pair up and wait on the side, taking turns entering the square to win the ball off the attackers.

The Attackers aim to keep possession for as long as possible while the defenders try to win possession or force the ball out. As soon as the Defenders win the ball they leave the square, another ball is passed into the Attackers and the next pair of Defenders enter.

Swap the teams once all pairs have defended or every 2 minutes.

◈ COACHES NOTES:

- **Well Weighted Passes** - make sure the players focus on the weight and accuracy of their passes so it doesn't put their teammate under pressure.

- **Ball Control** - When receiving a pass, can the players first touch be into space and away from the Defender? The player should take the ball on their back foot when possible so they can open their body up if needed and pass forward.

- **Awareness** - Players should be thinking what they will do before they receive the ball - what are the options? Can they see what players are open for the next pass? Can they move into space to make the area larger and therefore harder for the Defenders to press and shut them down?

- **Communication** - Do this by: Talking to teammates; Directing others using hand signals; Making eye contact with teammates.

☑ PROGRESSION:

- **Make it more competitive by timing how long the Attacking team can keep possession of the ball** until each pair has had a turn (go through two or three times if there is only a couple of pairs). The team of Attackers who keeps possession the longest wins.

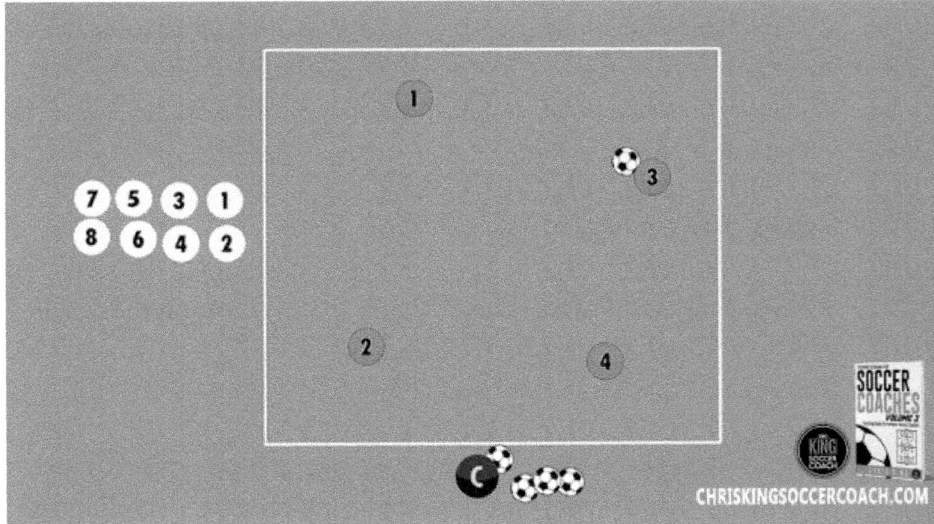

4 Attacking players start in the square and aim to keep possession. Defenders enter in pairs and try to win the ball. As soon as they have won the ball, they exit and a fresh pair come in.

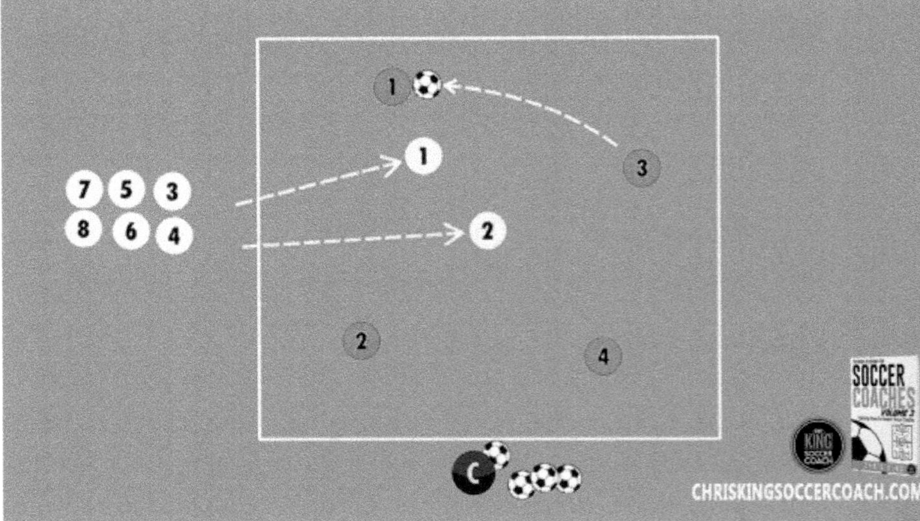

The two Defenders work together and press the area where the ball is. Here Yellow/Light #1 presses Red/Dark #1 who is about to take possession. And Yellow/Light #2 sticks close by and should try to block the passing lane back to Red/Dark #3 as well as the potential split pass to Red/Dark #4.

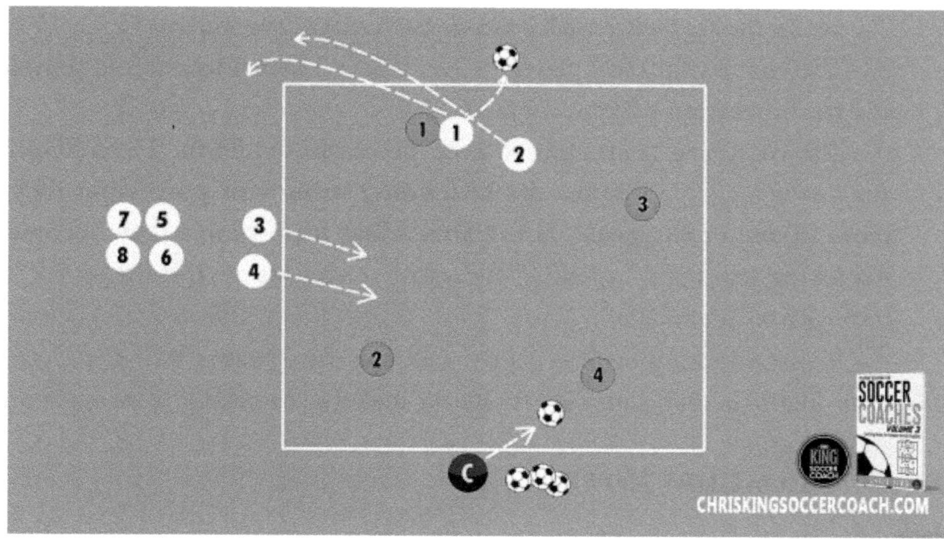

Red/Dark #1 dilly dallied on the ball and was caught in possession. Yellow/ Light #1 kicks the ball out and both Yellow/Light players leave the square. The coach feeds the Attackers a new ball as two new Defenders (Yellow/Light #3 and #4) enter.

SESSION 1 "POSSESSION UNDER PRESSURE"
DRILL B (THE DEVELOPMENT PHASE)
"TREAT IT LIKE GOLD "

PURPOSE:

- Keeping possession and composure under pressure.
- Good quality passing under pressure.
- Creating space.

SET UP:

- **12 Players (Alternatively 9 players with teams of 3)**
- 20x20 yard square
- 4 mini goals

THE DRILL:

Set up the area with small goals on each side of the square.

There are 3 teams of 4 players. 4 Attackers v 4 Defenders start in the middle and the other team waits to come on.

The Attacking team aims to keep possession while the Defending team aims to win the ball. **Once the Defending team wins possession they can score in any of the goals. If the Defending team scores they become the Attacking team** and the initial Attacking team goes off and the resting team comes on to defend.

If the Attacking team kicks the ball out they rotate off. If the Defensive team kicks the ball out they rotate off and the Attacking team stays on for another go.

◈ COACHES NOTES:

- High tempo! Make sure as soon as a ball goes out or a goal is scored teams are quickly rotating off and a new ball is fed to the Attacking team to start straight away.

- As one of my old teammates used to say "Treat the ball like gold!". It's not much fun chasing around after the ball, so when you have possession don't do stupid passes and give it away. Treat it like it's gold and no other player is going to get it off you.

☑ PROGRESSION:

- Defenders do a punishment if the Attackers can keep the ball for a certain amount of time or a certain number of passes.

- If it's too hard for the Attacking team, have a Joker as an extra Attacker who stays on the attacking team.

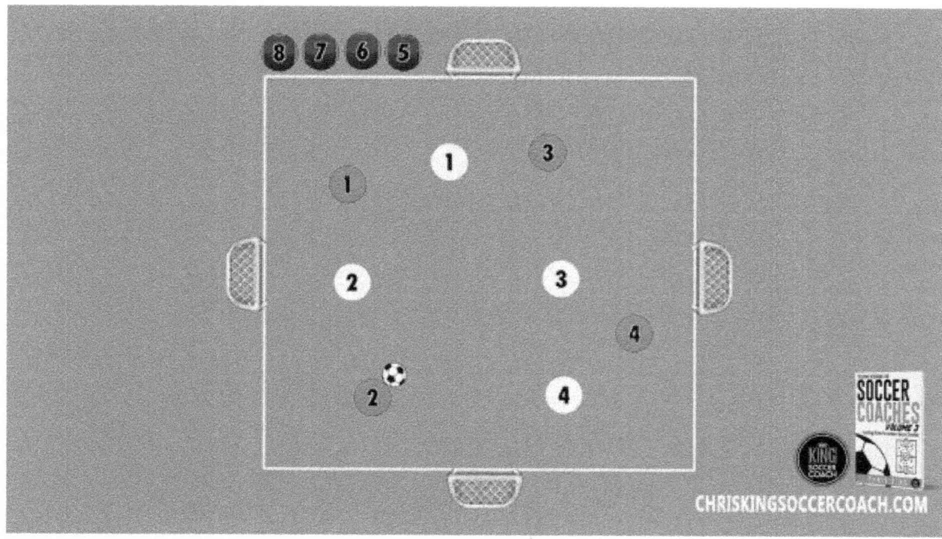

4 Attacking players (Red/Dark) aim to keep possession versus 4 Defenders (Yellow/Light) with the other team (Blue/Darker) resting. Once the Defenders win possession they can score in any goal.

As soon as the Defenders score, they become the Attacking team and the other team rotates in and the initial Attacking team is out.

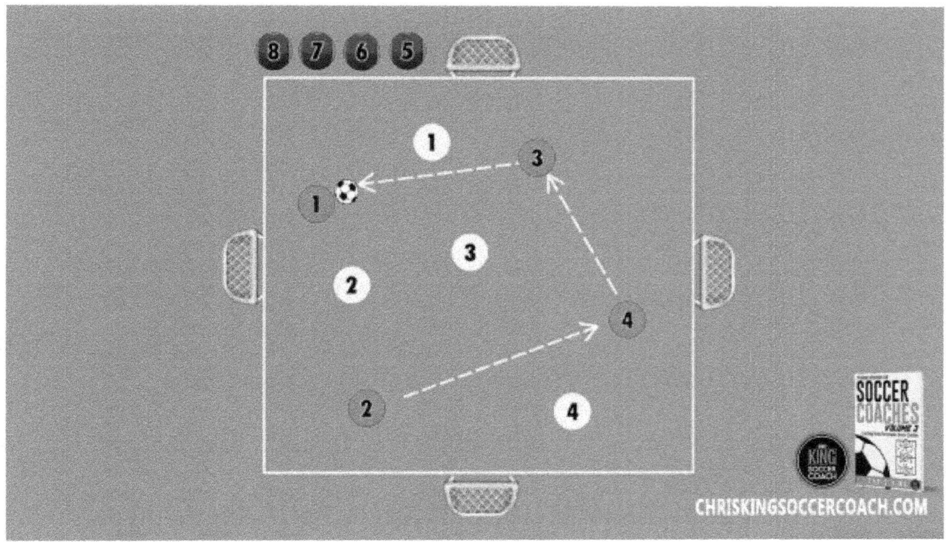

Red/Dark passes the ball around while Yellow/Light tries to press them to win possession and score.

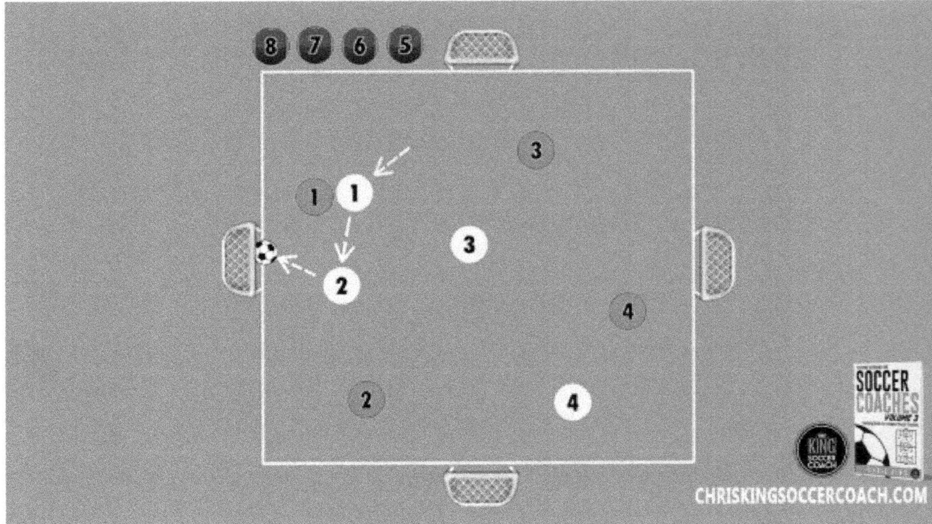

Red/Dark #1 has a bad touch and Yellow/Light #1 is on it in a flash. Yellow/Light #1 passes to #2 who scores in the mini goal.

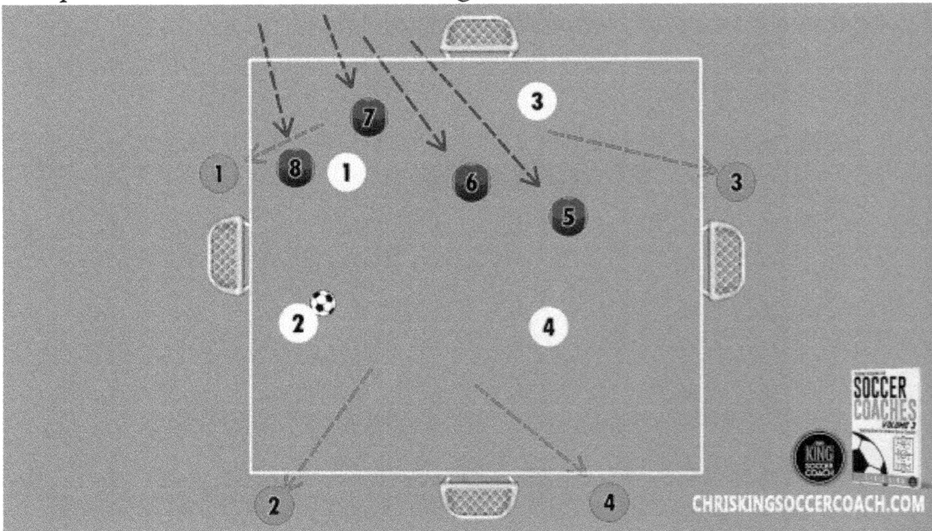

The Red/Dark team goes off, the Blue/Darker team comes on and the Yellow/Light team starts in possession.

SESSION 1 "POSSESSION UNDER PRESSURE"
DRILL C (THE GAME PHASE)
"CHAMPIONS LEAGUE FINAL"

◈ PURPOSE:

- The focus of this session, ***possession under pressure***, is worked on in this drill by getting the players to play "Champions League Final".

◈ SET UP:

- **10 Players + 2 Goalkeepers (Alternatively 8 players 4v4)**
- 20x30 yard square
- 2 large goals

◈ THE DRILL:

This is a game of 5v5 plus goalkeepers (if available, otherwise use a mannequin in the goal or mini goals). Once the first goal is scored, the team that has scored plays as if there is only 2 minutes left in the Champions League Final.

They are leading 1-0 and must try and just keep possession for the final 2 minutes.

Get them to focus on just possession without trying to score another goal. The other team piles on the pressure and tries to win possession back and score to equalise. If they can keep it for 2 minutes the other team has to do 20 push ups.

Once the other team wins possession and scores, reverse the roles.

<u>**Note:**</u> If a team scores but then the opposition wins the ball back within 2 minutes, it is just regular play until one of the teams scores again, then the 2 minutes starts again.

◈ COACHES NOTES:

- The team that is 1-0 up must show composure and not be scared to pass and shield the ball.

- Pass the ball as much as possible to move the Defenders around. If an Attacker is outnumbered or shut down quickly, they will have to show composure and shield the ball until they receive help from a teammate.

- Attackers should work in triangles/squares. The player on the ball should always have 2 options from teammates to pass to and 3 if possible.

- All basic skills that Rondos teach you come into effect in this drill:

Attackers: Pass to a teammates backfoot so they can play it forward or backwards; Passes should be well weighted so a teammate can pass it first time; Teammates should be working hard and moving into positions to receive the ball.

Defenders: Work as a team (hunt in pairs and other teammates block the passing lanes); Read the Attacker's intentions by looking at their body shape (are their hips open so they may be looking to pass forward?); Look at their eyes (have they given away their intentions by looking at where they intend to pass?).

☑ **PROGRESSION:**

- Make it maximum 2 touches so players don't dwell on the ball.

- If 2 minutes to keep possession is too long, make it 45 seconds or 1 minute.

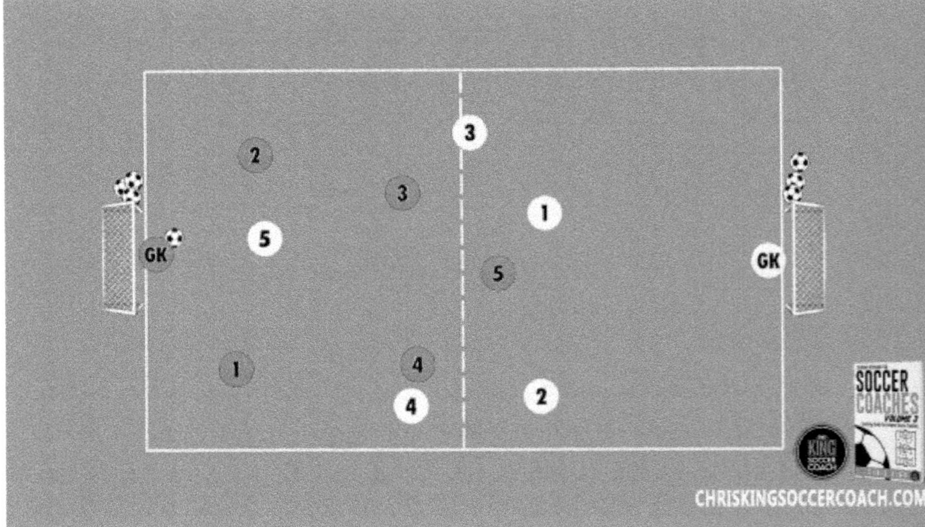

6v6 Champions League Final! Once a goal is scored, that team aims to keep possession for 2 minutes. The other team presses as hard as they can to win back possession and score themselves, then the roles reverse.

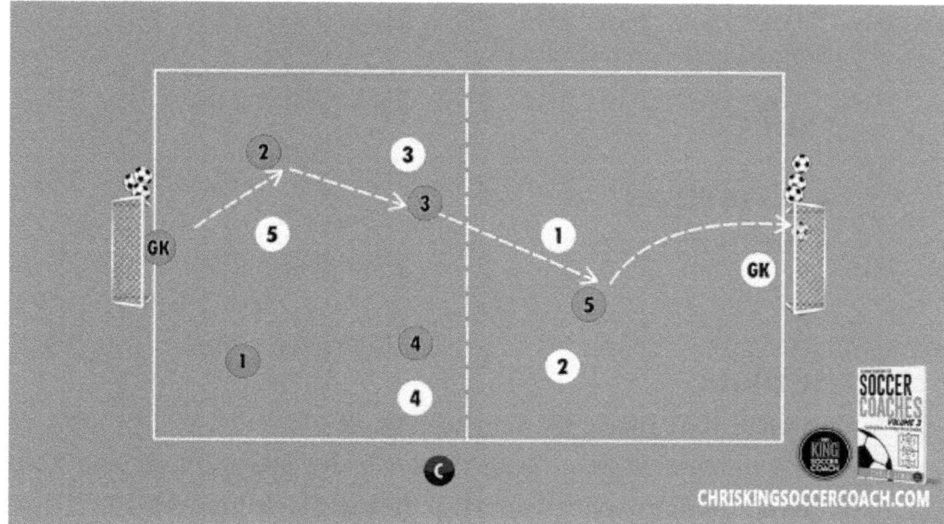

Red/Dark has scored first! There is only 2 minutes left in the final (the coach starts the stopwatch) so their aim is to keep possession. Yellows/Lights must put them under as much pressure as possible to try and win the ball back and score.

SESSION 2: INTERCEPTING A PASS

Session Objective:

Improving a players ability, when they aren't in possession, to read an opposition player's intention.

This will enable them to make interceptions (steal the ball) and start a counter attack while the opposition is out of shape.

SESSION 2 "INTERCEPTING A PASS"
DRILL A (THE LEARNING PHASE)
"3v1 INTERCEPT RONDO"

◈ PURPOSE:

- Intercepting ("stealing") the ball to win back possession.
- Reading/anticipating the play.
- Starting the counter attack.

◈ SET UP:

- **8 to 16 Players**
- 10x10 yard square

◈ THE DRILL:

In a small 10v10 area play 3v1 keepings off.

This is intense work so swap the Defender every minute and keep the Attackers to 2 touch maximum to keep the ball moving quickly.

Remember to coach the topics under the "Coaches Notes" section (Defenders should be looking at the Attacker's eyes, head movement and body shape to read their intentions).

How many times can the Defender get an intercept in a minute? Count them up and see who gets the most after everyone has Defended.

Or alternatively, the Attackers get 1 point for every 5 passes in a row and the Defender gets 1 point for forcing the ball out and **2 points for stealing the ball**.

At the end of each minute, count up the points and whoever has the least amount of points out of the Attackers or the Defender do a quick punishment (ie 5 push ups; 5 sit ups).

◈ COACHES NOTES:

- **Anticipate the pass** – Does the player with the ball give away their intentions by where their eyes are looking; their head movements; or the shape of their hips (if their hips are open they may be looking to pass forward. If their hips are closed chances are they are intending to pass back in the direction the ball came from)?

• **Defensive set up** - Apply pressure in the right areas/sides so as to make the attacking team's movements predictable. For example, force a player onto their weaker foot. Or try and press a player into a corner so they only have one option to pass out to which makes it predictable.

• Also, **can the Defender "fake out" the Attackers**? For example, a Defender should pretend to commit to going to one side but quickly adjust to the other side as the Attacker is about to pass (similar to what a goalkeeper tries to do on a penalty).

☑ **PROGRESSION:**

• Make it 1 touch so the Defender has more opportunities to win the ball.

• Make the square larger or smaller depending on how hard it is for the Defender to win the ball.

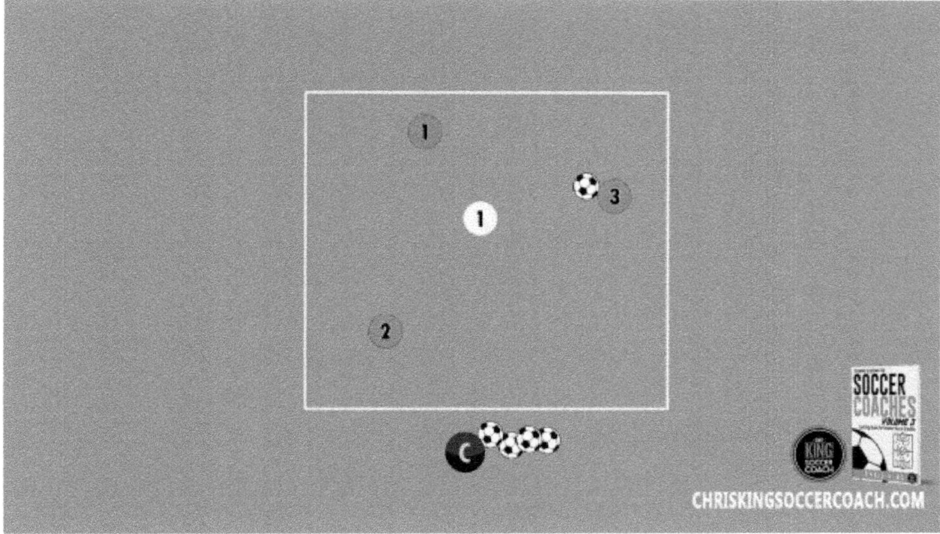

3 Reds/Dark v 1 Yellow/Light. Reds/Dark aim to keep possession. How many times can the Defender intercept the ball in 1 minute? Swap roles after a minute and keep count of which player gets the most intercepts.

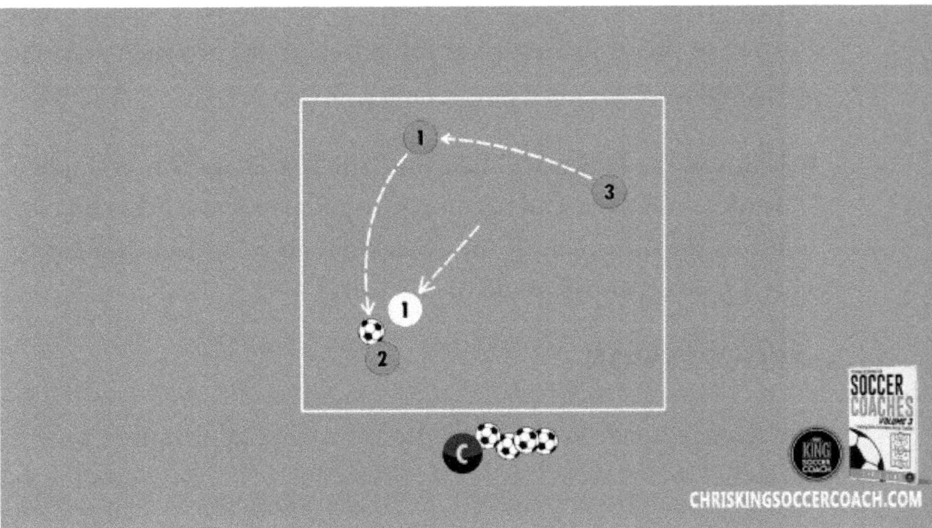

Reds/Dark spread out so it is hard for the Yellow/Light Defender to intercept the ball. Yellow/Light presses, trying to put pressure on the player in possession so they make a bad pass or don't control it properly and then they can pounce.

SESSION 2 "INTERCEPTING A PASS"
DRILL B (THE DEVELOPMENT PHASE)
"SEND IN THE TROOPS "

PURPOSE:

- Same as Drill 1 but working with a teammate so players learn how to press together to intercept a pass.
- Intercepting ("stealing") the ball to win possession.
- Reading/anticipating the play.
- Starting a counter attack.

SET UP:

- **8 Players (Alternatively up to 12 Players, have an even amount on each team).**

- 20x30 yard square

◈ **THE DRILL:**

Set up a 20x30 yard pitch with two halves.

4 Red players in one half and 4 Yellow players in the other (if there are more players, simply add 1 or 2 to each team. If there are uneven numbers use a "Joker" - who is simply a player who plays with the team in possession).

The Red team starts with the ball and 2 Yellow players run into the other half to try and win the ball in a 4v2 situation. Once they win it, they must pass it back to their teammates in the other half. They then return to their half and 2 players from the Red team go to the other half to try and win possession.

Scoring: 5 passes = 1 goal. At the end of 5 minutes count up who has the most.

◈ **COACHES NOTES:**

- Some key points to focus on are for the 2 players to work together - they should close down space together and not be too far apart. If they spread out the opposition can pick them off. So they should be close enough to each other that they can try and intercept passes between them.

- And remember to use the skills learnt from the first drill: Where is the Attacker looking to pass the ball (what are their eyes or head movement)? Are their hips open (showing an intent to pass forward)?

☑ **PROGRESSION:**

- If it's too easy for the Defenders, only send 1 Defender over and then every 5 passes the Attacking team makes, send over another Defender.

- If it's too easy for the Attackers, limit their touches to 1 or 2 touch.

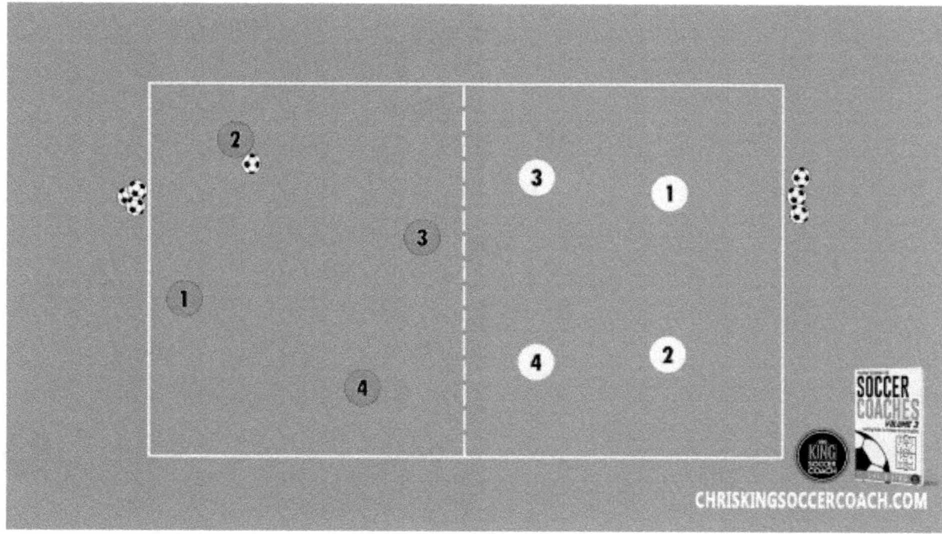

4v4. Reds/Dark start with possession and as soon as they make their first pass, two Yellows/Light race over to try and win possession. Once they win possession they try to pass it back to their teammates and the roles of the team reverse (ie 4 Yellows/Light try and keep it off 2 Red/Dark).

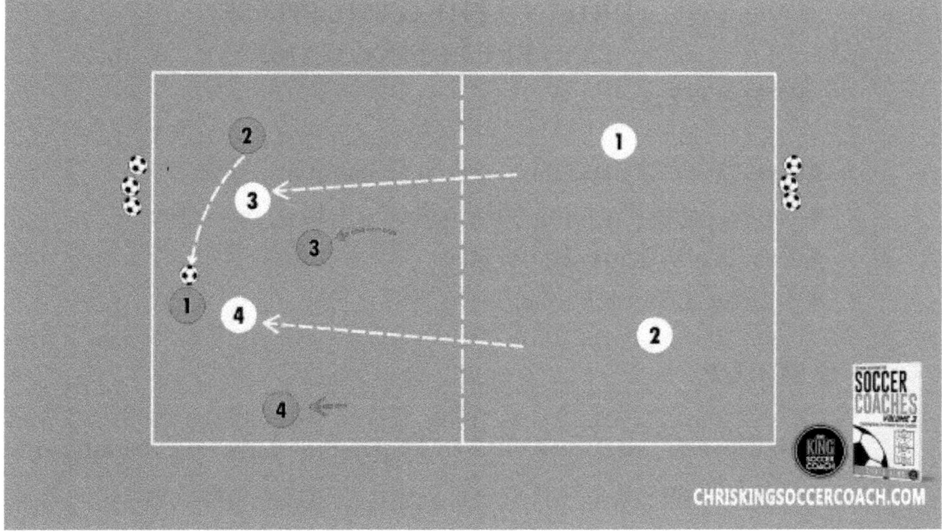

Red/Dark makes the first pass so two Yellows/Light race over to try and win possession as quickly as possible. The Reds/Dark move into positions where they can receive the ball to support their teammate.

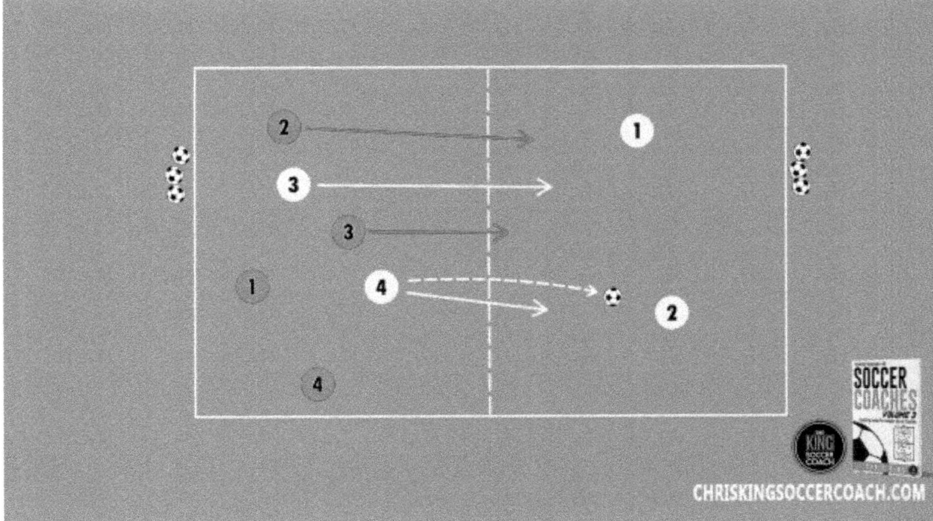

Here Yellow/Light #4 has won possession. They pass the ball back across to their teammates and both players race back to help keep possession in their half. Two Red/Dark players (#2 & #3) come across to try and win possession.

SESSION 2 "INTERCEPTING A PASS" DRILL C (THE GAME PHASE) "INTERCEPTING GAME"

◈ **PURPOSE:**

- Same as Drill 1 and 2 but now it's a game situation.
- Intercepting ("stealing") the ball to win back possession.
- Reading/anticipating the play.
- Starting a counter attack.

◈ **SET UP:**

- **10 Players (Alternatively 8 to 12 players - have an even amount on each team)**

- 30x40 yard square

- 2 Large goals

⯑ THE DRILL:

A simple progression from the first two drills but now it's in a more match like situation.

Set up a 30x40 yard pitch with goals at each end.

An even amount of players on each team (5v5 ideally). Limit the play to 1 and 2 touches so that it will give players plenty of opportunities to intercept the ball.

A goal is achieved by either scoring in the goal or 3 intercepts (make sure to keep count every time there is a clear interception from a pass).

⯑ COACHES NOTES:

- Make sure players are focussed on what they learnt in the first two drills: **Anticipate the pass** – Does the player with the ball give away their intentions by where their eyes are looking; their head movements/ or the shape of their hips (if their hips are open they may be looking to pass forward. If their hips are closed chances are they are intending to pass back in the direction the ball came from)?

- **Defensive set up** - Apply pressure in the right areas/sides so as to make the attacking team's movements predictable. Plus communicate with team mates to be organised defensively.

- Don't just think "Well Done!" once you win it - **use a quick pass to start a counter attack.**

- Also, **can the Defender "fake out" the Attackers**? For example, a Defender should pretend to commit to going to one side but quickly adjust to the other side as the Attacker is about to pass.

☑ PROGRESSION:

- If you have a large squad, play an 11 v 11 and use the same rules (ie 3 intercepts equals a goal). But keep it to a smaller area than a full pitch to allow plenty of opportunities for interceptions.

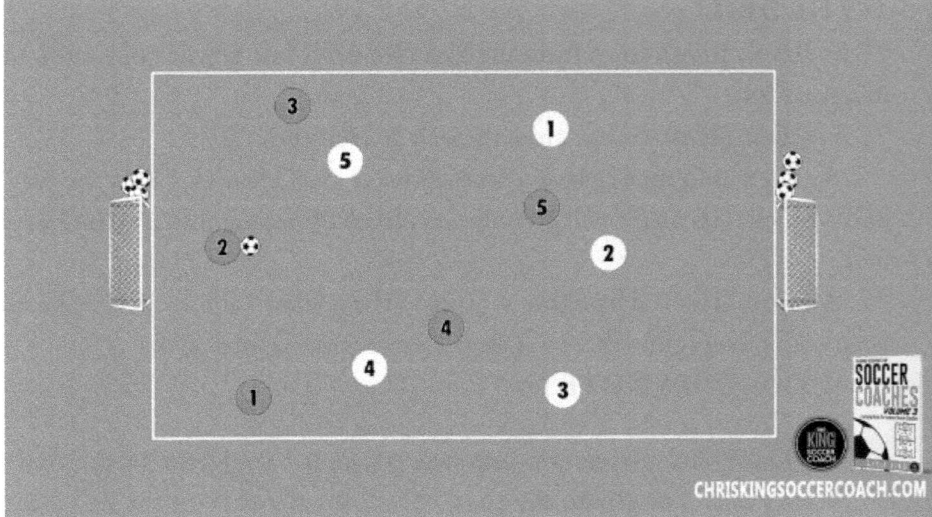

5v5 small sided game. Limit it to 1 or 2 touches so there are lots of chances for players to intercept the ball. 3 intercepts add up to one goal.

SESSION 3: SWITCH THE PLAY

Session Objective:

To improve players' awareness to switch the play. This session will put players in situations so they know when is a good opportunity to switch the play (ie change the direction of the play). This will be achieved by focussing on players body shape and making space.

SESSION 3 "SWITCH THE PLAY"
DRILL A (THE LEARNING PHASE)
"SWITCHING BASICS"

� PURPOSE:

- Getting players used to the idea of opening the play up by switching it to the opposite side. Players work on body shape and taking the ball on their back foot.

◈ SET UP:

- **6 Players (7 or 8 players: Add in passive Defenders in the centre to put some pressure on the middle players. 3 Players: Only have one set of 3 players in the square)**

- 20x20 yard square

◈ THE DRILL:

Create a 20x20 yard square.

Split the 6 players into 2 groups of 3.

1 Player from each team starts in the middle with the other 2 at opposite sides of the square.

Player 1 passes to their teammate in the middle (Player 2) and follows their pass (they will end up in the middle). Player 2 controls the ball on the turn (taking it on their back foot [this is their foot furthest from where the ball is coming from]) and passes to Player 3. Player 2 rotates out from where they received the pass (Player 1).

Next, Player 3 passes to Player 2 who is now in the middle and follows the ball in. Player 2 turns and passes back to Player 1 who is on the outside and turns back and goes out to the other side.

Play for 2 minutes, rest for 30 seconds and go again.

I admit that may sound a bit confusing, so if you are in doubt just read this summarisation:

Summarisation - Outside Players: Passes the ball to the middle player and follows the pass to become the middle player.

Summarisation - Middle Player: Receives the ball from one side, passes to the other side, rotates out from where the pass came.

◈ COACHES NOTES:

• The focus of this session is the switch of play. So we want the middle player to be head checking (looking around to see where they will pass it next) before they receive the ball.

• The middle player should be taking a step away from the ball just before it is passed. Then they can come towards and meet the ball. If this was in a game they would have created a yard by pushing against the player marking them and then going back towards the ball. Plus they aren't flat footed.

• The middle player should take the ball on their back foot (furthest from where the ball is passed from). This way they are able to naturally pass forward as their body is open.

• **Summarisation of key points for the middle player: 1.** Head check before the ball is passed. **2.** Step away and then back towards the ball just as it is passed. **3.** Take the ball on the back foot.

• Outside players should be passing to the middle players' back foot so they can pass forward easily. The middle player should be pointing down to the ground to show the passer the area where they want to receive the ball. You can never have enough physical and verbal communication. Get your players talking, pointing and organising as much as possible! It all adds up on a game day and gets players in correct positions plus it helps the younger players on the team.

☑ **PROGRESSION:**

• Add a passive defender in the middle to put pressure on the middle player. No actual tackling but some body pressure to make it more match realistic.

• If players are struggling, make the area slightly bigger so they have more time to receive the ball or get them to slow the passes down.

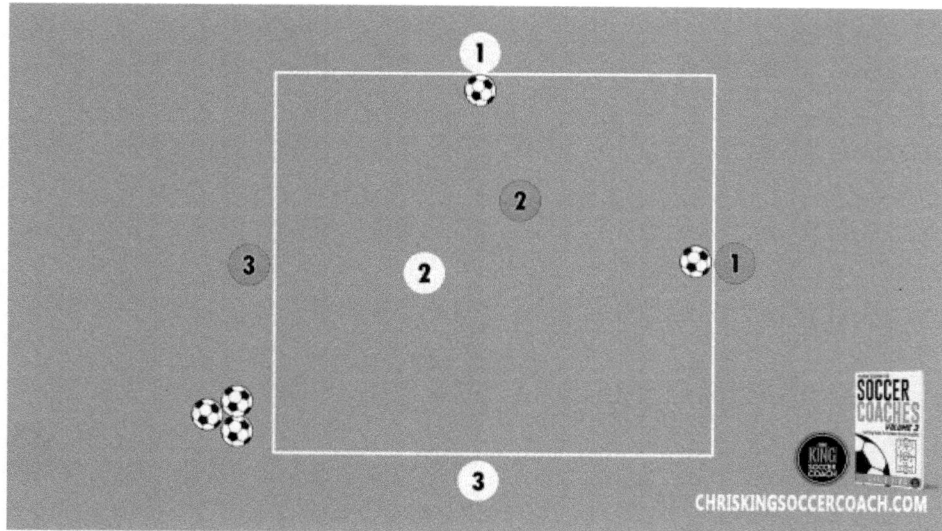

3 Reds/Dark work together at the same time as the 3 Yellows/Light. Players must be aware so as they don't run into each other in the middle or the balls don't collide.

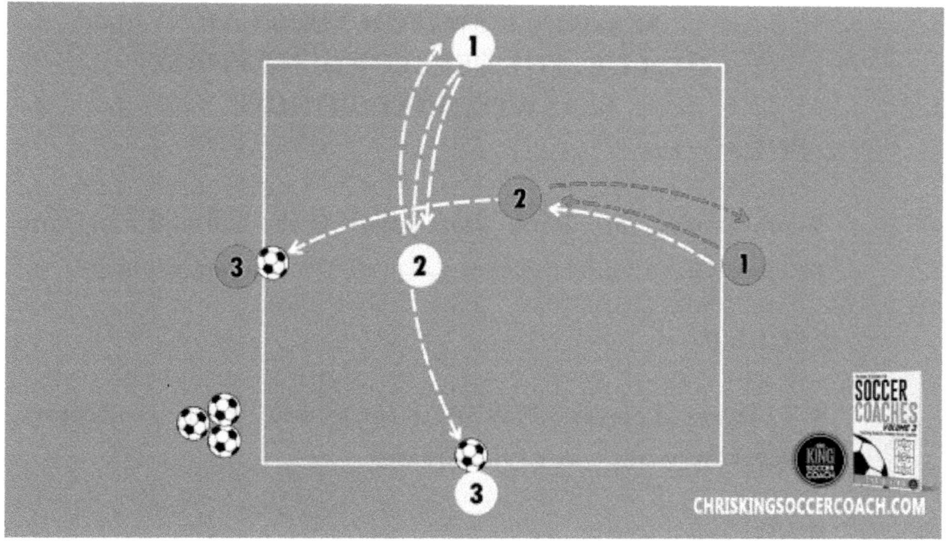

Here both #1's pass to the centre players (#2's). The centre player turns on the ball and passes out to #3. At the same time #1's follow their pass in and become the centre player. #2's turn back once they have passed and take the place of where the initial pass came from (#1's spot).

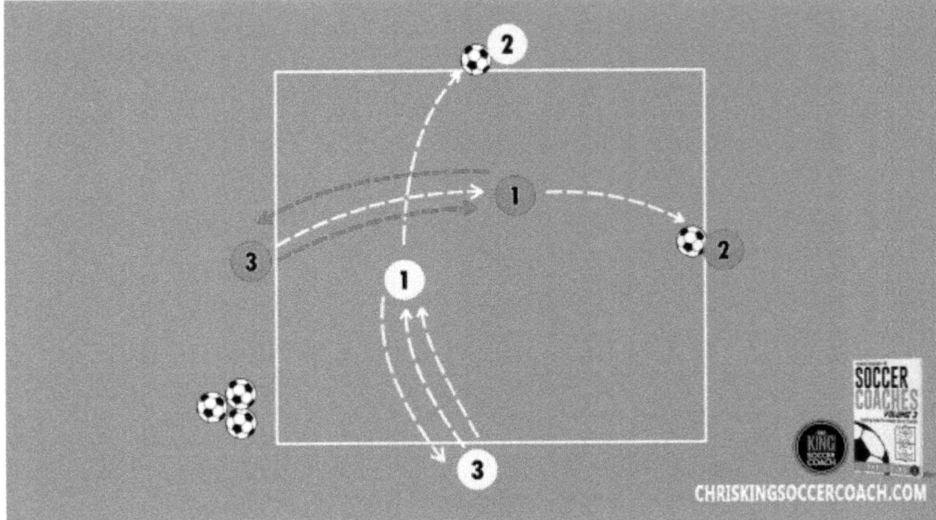

Once #3 receives the ball, they pass it into the middle to #1. Who turns on the ball and passes it out the other side to #2. #3 follows their pass into the middle and #1 turns and goes out where the initial pass came from (#3's spot).

SESSION 3 "SWITCH THE PLAY" DRILL B (THE DEVELOPMENT PHASE) "5v2 SWITCHING RONDO"

◈ PURPOSE:

- Working on the central player receiving the ball under pressure and passing out in the opposite direction (switching the play).

◈ SET UP:

- **7 Players (8 players: Play 2v2 in the middle. 6 players: Remove a player from one side of the square)**

- 15x15 yard square

◈ THE DRILL:

Set up a 15x15 yard square.

It is 5v2. 4 players are around the sides of the square with 1 teammate inside the square. 2 Defenders are also inside the square.

Attackers must pass the ball around or through the square. If they pass to their teammate in the middle they receive 1 point. If they make 10 passes in a row they receive 1 point.

If the Defenders win the ball, they keep possession 2v1 against the middle player. Every 5 passes they make is a point. After 10 passes, an Attackers teammate can enter the square to help win back possession. Once the middle player/s win back possession, reset and start again.

⛗ COACHES NOTES:

- The coaches notes are similar to the first drill because we still want to work on body shape so that players can switch the play. Get the players to focus on:

- **We want the middle player to be head checking** (looking around to see where they will pass it next) before they receive the ball.

- **The middle player should be taking the ball on their back foot when possible** (they will be under pressure so they may have to take it on their nearest foot sometimes to protect the ball against the 2 Defenders)

- **The outside players should constantly move into good positions** to present themselves as an option to be passed to.

☑ PROGRESSION:

- If the players are skilled enough, make it 1 or 2 touch maximum. This will improve their head checking as they will have to know ahead of receiving the ball where the Defenders and space are. It will also greatly improve their overall sharpness.

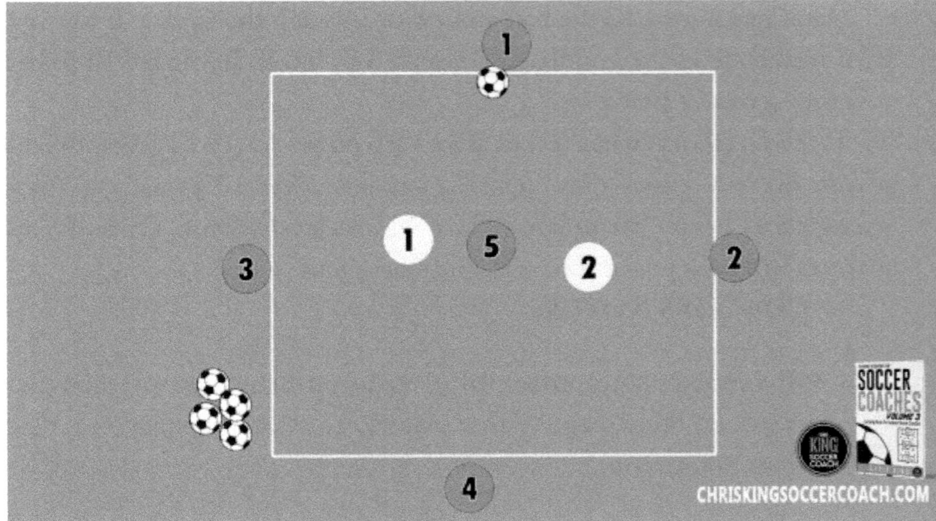

5 Red/Dark players are aiming to keep possession v 2 Yellows/Light. 1 point for a pass to the centre player (Red/Dark #5) and 1 point for 10 passes in a row. If Yellow/Light win the ball, they keep possession 2v1 until Red/Dark #5 can win the ball back.

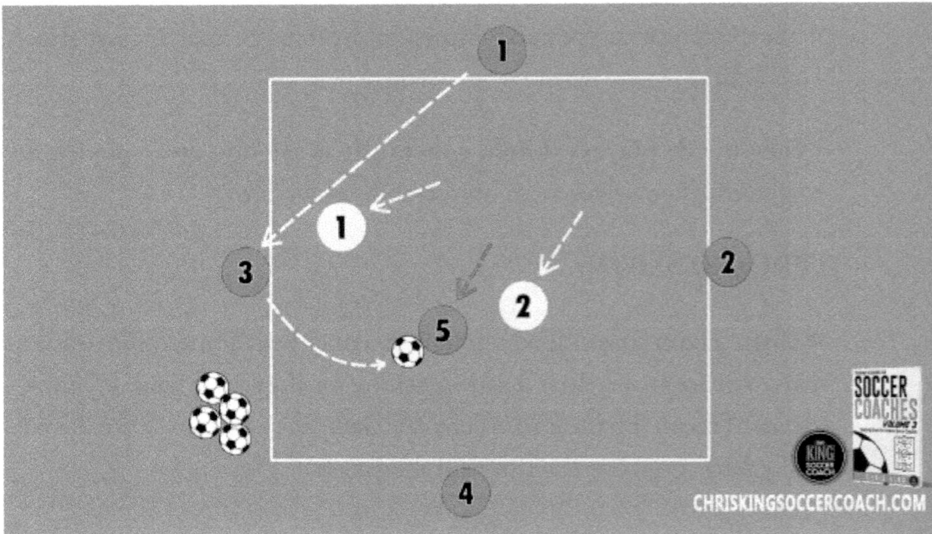

Here Reds/Dark have passed it successfully to the middle player (Red/Dark #5) so they get 1 point.

SESSION 3 "SWITCH THE PLAY" DRILL C (THE GAME PHASE) "HALF PITCH GAME"

◈ PURPOSE:

- To use the switch of play in a game situation to find space and unbalance the opposition.

◈ SET UP:

- **16 Players + 2 Goalkeepers (Alternatively 12 to 18 outfield players. Remove or add players into the central area as needed).**
- ½ pitch
- 2 Large goals

◈ THE DRILL:

To finish the switch of play session, here we bring it all together in a large game situation.

It is 7v7 outfield players, 2 Jokers + 2 Goalkeepers (start as a 1-3-2-2 formation plus the 2 Jokers who play on the team in possession). Use half a pitch (smaller area for less numbers and use ⅔ a pitch for 9v9+2 or more players).

Set up two channels down each side with 1 Joker in each (remember, Jokers play for the team in possession). This will encourage players to switch the ball to the outside channels, which is usually where the space is when looking at switching the play.

Play starts from the goalkeepers (no throw-ins). The team that scores gets to keep possession.

◈ COACHES NOTES:

- Encourage fast passing sideways and into the midfield to move the opposition around. This will create space and opportunities to switch the play.

• Make sure to focus on the skills from the previous drills: **1.** Head checking to see where the options to switch to are; **2.** Passing to a player's back foot; **3.** The player receiving the ball takes it on their back foot so they can go out the furthest side.

• Make sure the opposition are pressing so it puts the Defense under pressure so they can practise switching under pressure situations.

• Players should be communicating and telling each other when the switch is on.

☑ **PROGRESSION:**

• Remove the channels and play a regular game but make sure to still encourage the switch of play to the flanks.

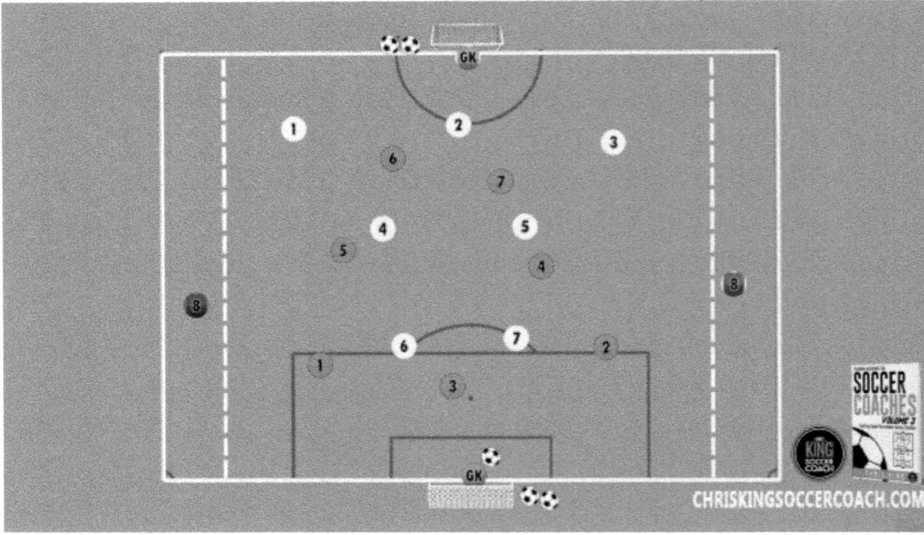

7v7. 1-3-2-2 formation with 2 Jokers in the channels. Play starts from the goalkeepers and the team in possession should be passing quickly, moving the ball and looking for opportunities to switch the ball out to the other side.

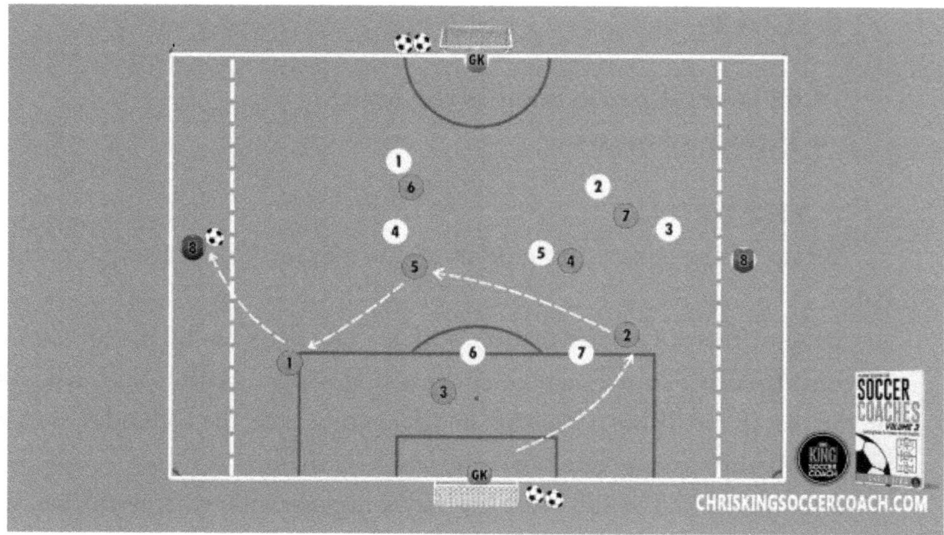

Play starts with the goalkeeper passing out to the right fullback (Red/Dark #2). The opposition (Yellow/Light) pushes across to press, so this opens up space on the left. Through quick passing, the Red/Dark team can switch the play through the midfield and out to the Joker on the left wing. This will have opened up space and makes a great opportunity to put a dangerous ball in.

SESSION 4: DEFENDING 1v1

<u>**Session Objective:**</u>

To improve players ability to defend 1v1 in different situations.

SESSION 4 "DEFENDING 1v1"

DRILL A (THE LEARNING PHASE)

" 1v1 KEEPING POSSESSION "

⟐ PURPOSE:

- Defenders being able to keep the ball 1v1 until help arrives.

⟐ SET UP:

- **6 Players (Up to as many as you want)**
- **25x25 yard square**

⟐ THE DRILL:

Set up a large square and pair off all the players. One player per pair has a ball.

Imagine this is a game situation, with a Defender who has possession in the bottom defensive corner against an attacking winger. Rather than risk taking on the player and losing possession in a dangerous area, the Defender must keep possession until a teammate can come and help them.

So in this drill, the aim is for the player in possession to keep the ball while the opponent tries to win possession (and then keep it themselves).

Play for 1 minute and whoever has the ball at the end of the minute wins the round. Play 3 rounds and swap who starts with the ball each round.

Players get 1 point for winning each round or 4 points if they win all 3 rounds. First player to 8 points wins.

After 3 rounds, swap opponents.

⟐ COACHES NOTES:

- Can the player with the ball make their centre of gravity lower by slightly bending at the knees? This will provide a solid base so they can't be knocked off the ball.

- Other key points are: **Keep the ball on the foot furthest** from where the opponent is; **Keep the arms bent out** from the body (like chicken wings) to make your body bigger; **Body position should be slightly side on** (so the opposition player can't reach the ball through or around the legs); If there is body contact **slightly lean back into the other player**.

- **Tip to win the possession**: If you can get side on to the player in possession, can you "step across" the ball to win the ball?

- So, for example, if Player 1 was in possession and they were shoulder to shoulder with Player 2 (Player 1's right shoulder was against Player 2's left shoulder), can Player 2 step across with their left leg and use their bum to get Player 1 out of the way?Then they have their body over the ball and can protect it themselves. It is all about body strength and timing.

☑ PROGRESSION:

● Players don't work in pairs but instead half the players have a ball and the other half can tackle and win possession off any player in the square. So players in possession have to have their wits about them as someone might come in from any angle. Play for 1 minute and the players that have a ball at the end get a point.

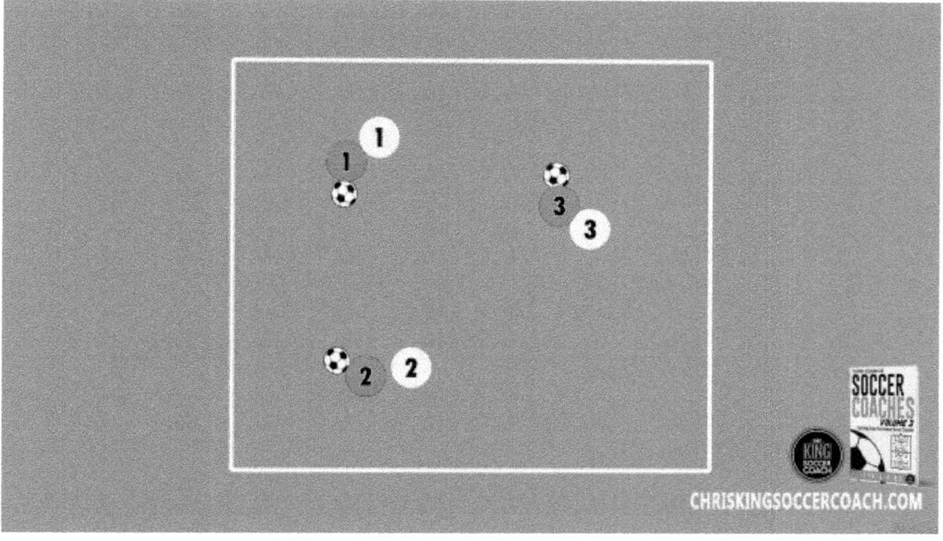

Players pair off and play 1v1 trying to keep possession. Play for 1 minute and whoever has possession at the end of 1 minute scores 1 point. Play 3 rounds then swap opponents.

Players should dribble, shield, hold the opponent off with body strength and do whatever they can to keep possession. The ball should be kept on the furthest side to the opponent so the ball can't be reached.

Red/Dark #1 and #2 are keeping possession well. But Yellow/Light #3 has won possession off Red/Dark #3, so Yellow/Light #3 now tries to keep possession until the minute is up.

SESSION 4 "DEFENDING 1v1"
DRILL B (THE DEVELOPMENT PHASE)
" 1v1 MINI GOALS "

◈ PURPOSE:

- Players practise Attacking and Defending in a 1v1 situation. Can Defenders not get scored on? Plus can Defenders win possession and dribble out of trouble?

◈ SET UP:

- **8 Players (If more players set up 1 mini goal per extra pair. If less players remove a mini goal.)**

- 4 Mini goal
- Large 40x40 yard square with 10x10 square inside it

◈ THE DRILL:

Set up a large 40x40 yard square with a 10x10 yard square marked out in the middle.

4 mini goals on each side of the large square.

Pair off the players and one from each pair starts in the middle square with a ball. Their opponent defends a mini goal each.

Attackers dribble out of the square and try to score. If they score, they remain as the Attacker and go back to the middle and go again! If the Defender wins the ball they can either shield it for 10 seconds or dribble it back to the centre square to become the Attacker.

There is a 30 second limit for the Attacker to score a goal. If they don't score in that time, swap roles.

Rotate the Defenders around the square every few minutes so the players are versing different opponents.

◈ COACHES NOTES:

- This drill helps the Defenders learn to read the Attackers intentions. The Attackers will want to go at pace so they can hopefully dribble past the Defender. So to counteract this, remind the Defenders to do these things:

Get slightly side on and show the Attacker away from goal. For example, if the Defender is slightly side-on with their right shoulder slightly facing the Attacker, they want the Attacker to go down to the left side (which should be away from goal, therefore making it harder to score).

Get out to the Attacker and set themselves. Defenders shouldn't stand close to the goal and wait for the Attacker! They should get further out to give themselves the best chance to stop them (if the Attacker gets past the Defender, they may still be able to get back and recover). Defenders shouldn't rush out like an idiot and over commit - sprint out and then as they get close, slow down and get side on, ready to jockey.

Jockey! This means holding the player where they are - not over committing and getting skinned! Defenders set themselves and slow down the Attacker and don't let them past. Make themselves hard and annoying to get past.

Can they get the Attacker facing away from goal? If they can slow the Attacker down, get touch tight and make them face away from goal.

☑ **PROGRESSION:**

- Attackers can go and attack a different goal. The defender has to quickly adjust and go and protect the other goal.

- Make it a 20 second limit per Attack so there is urgency in the play.

- Remove two balls and play 2v2. Attackers can go to any goal which will make the Defenders have to constantly adjust, recover, communicate and jockey the player or win the ball.

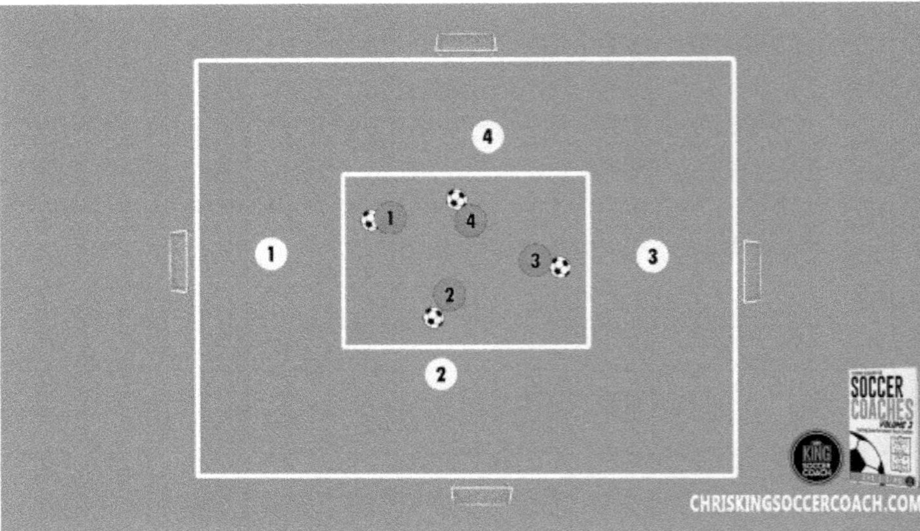

Players pair off. Attackers start in the middle square. They try to dribble past and score against a Defender. If they score they remain as the Attacker. If the Defender wins the ball and keeps it for 10 seconds or dribbles into the centre square they become the Attacker.

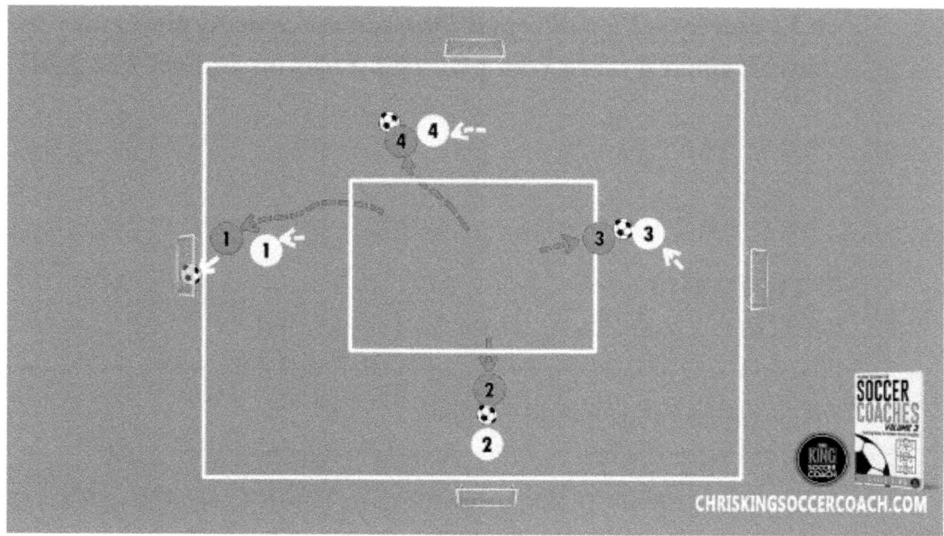

Red/Dark #1 *has dribbled at pace and gone past their Defender and scored.*

Red/Dark #2 *has done well and gone quickly at their Defender but must now pick a side to go past the Defender. They shouldn't slow down as this will make it easier for the Defender to jockey them or win the ball.*

Red/Dark #3 *was slow out of the blocks and had a bad touch. This allowed Yellow/Light #3 to pounce and win the ball.*

Red/Dark #4 *has been pushed wide by the Defender. It will be hard to score from here.*

SESSION 4 "DEFENDING 1v1"
DRILL C (THE GAME PHASE)
" 1v1 LARGE GOALS "

◈ PURPOSE:

- Defenders must use their 1v1 skills learnt in the previous two drills. They must jockey, hold, tackle, do whatever they can to delay the Attacker and stop them getting a shot on goal.

◈ SET UP:

- **12 Players + 2 Goalkeepers (You can use as many players as you have. If you only have a few players just use one end and one goal)**

- ⅓ or ½ a pitch

- 2 large goals

◈ THE DRILL:

Use ⅓ to ½ a pitch. Set up a large goal at each end.

Place a cone 20 yards out from each goal. One Defender starts on the cone and the rest are waiting behind the goal.

Place a cone at the halfway line. Attackers start here with a ball.

As soon as a Defender is on the cone the Attacker can start. They have 20 seconds to score. If they score, the Defender does 5 push ups.

If the Defender can jockey and stop them from getting a good shot off on target, the Attacker does 5 push ups.

If there is a shot but no goal, there are no push ups to either player.

As soon as there is a goal or the 20 seconds are up that round finishes and the next Defender races out to the cone and the next Attacker can start.

◈ COACHES NOTES:

- Make sure the Defensive player is implementing the skills they have learnt in the previous drills:

1. They should be **getting out to the Attacker as soon as possible** to keep them as far away from goal as they can.
2. They should be setting themselves with **slightly bent knees and slightly side on** (showing and guiding the Attacker away from goal and into the channels).
3. If they slow the Attacker down, **can they then get touch tight and get the Attacker facing away from goal or win the ball?**
4. Defenders should be improving their footwork, defensive angles (keeping between the opponent and the goal), timing of tackles and stealing the ball when the opportunity arises.

☑ PROGRESSION:

- Make it 2 Attackers v 2 Defenders.

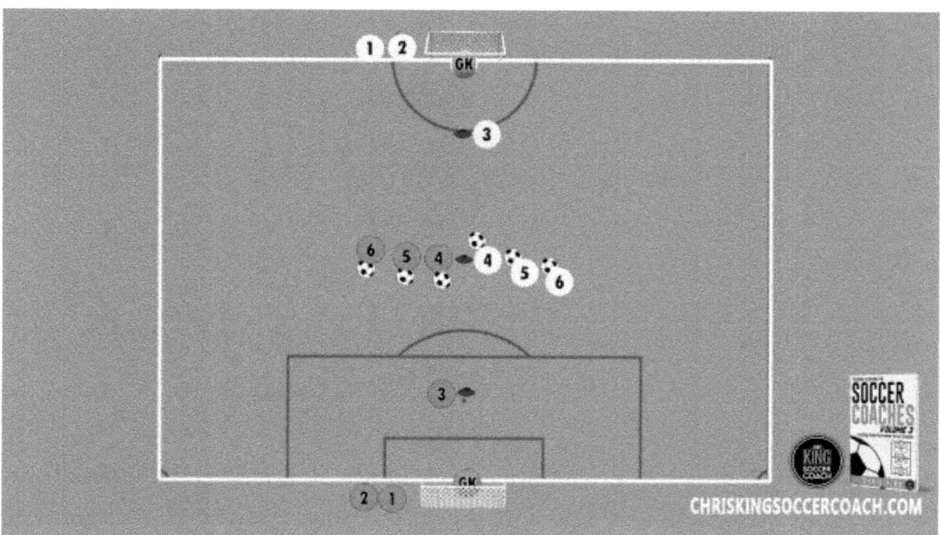

1v1. The Attacker starts on the centre cone, the Defender starts on the cone near the penalty spot.

If the Attacker scores the Defender does 5 push ups. If the Defender can stop the Attacker getting a shot on target the Attacker does 5 push ups.

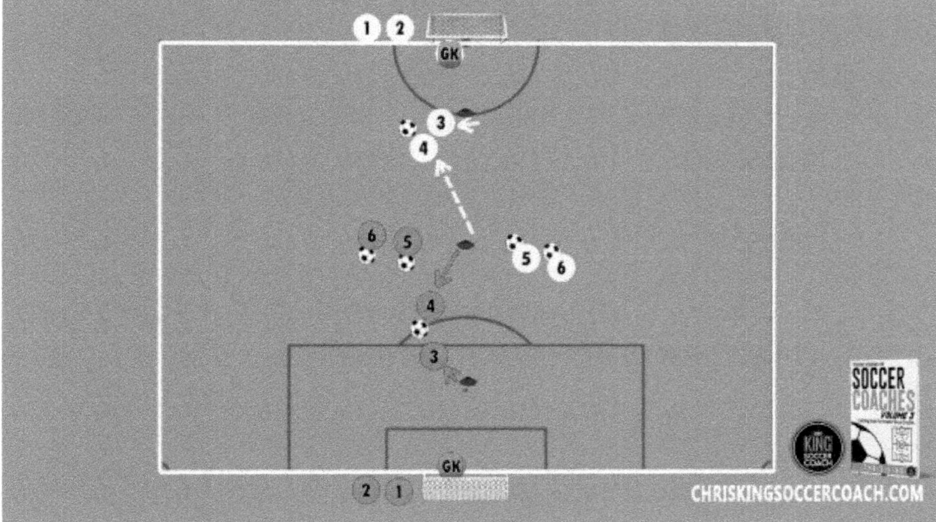

As soon as there is a Defender on the cone the Attacker can start. Once the play is over a new Defender sprints out to the cone and the next attack starts. Make sure the Defenders are using all the skills they have been working on in the previous two drills.

SESSION 5: ESSENTIAL SKILLS FOR GOALKEEPERS

Session Objective:

To improve the goalkeepers key skills: Catching; Distribution; and Passing with their Defenders. A lot of time in grassroots soccer goalkeepers aren't given specialty training. So this session aims to help them improve the main skills they use throughout a game.

SESSION 5 "ESSENTIAL SKILLS FOR GOALKEEPERS"

DRILL A (THE LEARNING PHASE)

" CATCHING & QUICK DISTRIBUTION "

◈ PURPOSE:

- To work on the goalkeepers catching from crosses and quick distribution.

◈ SET UP:

- **2 Players + 2 Goalkeepers (Alternatively 3 or 4 goalkeepers and 4 players - see progression for details)**
- ⅓ or ½ a pitch
- 2 large goals + 4 mini goals
- 4 mannequins (or poles)

◈ THE DRILL:

Set up half a pitch split in half with goals at either end.

1 goalkeeper in each goal. 1 player on either side of the halfway line with lots of balls each and a mini goal next to them.

2 other mini goals back to back at the halfway point.

2 mannequins (or poles if no mannequins) 5 yards either side of the penalty spot.

The 2 players cross a ball each into the penalty area (aiming in between the two mannequins).

The goalkeeper comes out and claims the ball, catching above their head.

As soon as they have caught the ball they run to the edge of the box and practise their distribution by hand. They throw the ball, with power, aiming for one of the mini goals. After 10 crosses whichever goalkeeper has successfully cleanly caught (minus one goal if they drop a ball) and thrown the most balls into the mini goal wins.

Note: Change the position of the mini-goals every few run throughs so the goalkeepers can practise throwing different distances and angles. Also practise some long kicks to the other goalkeeper in between rounds.

◈ COACHES NOTES:

- Focus on the goalkeeper coming for the ball with confidence. They should attack the ball and jump and catch it at its highest point (therefore an Attacker can't out jump them). They should have a knee up to protect themselves.

- Once they have caught the ball their attention should turn to if they can quickly distribute the ball to start an attack. They should hold the ball safely to their chest while they run towards the edge of the box looking for where to throw the ball (in this case the mini goal!).

- The throwing technique should be like a fast bowler in cricket or a javelin thrower. The ball should be pinned against the inside of the forearm and then bring the arm back behind the body. Then it should come over the shoulder and be released in front of the body.

The other arm should be used as a guide and point towards the target and they should step into the throw (to create power).

☑ **PROGRESSION:**

● If you have more than 2 goalkeepers, put the extra ones in the penalty area to act as an Attacker to put pressure on the other goalkeeper as the ball comes in. Then swap roles.

● Put other mini goals or targets (a mannequin, pole, bin) in different areas and get the goalkeepers to aim for these as well (you might have a target closer or to the side so they can practise doing an under arm or side arm throw).

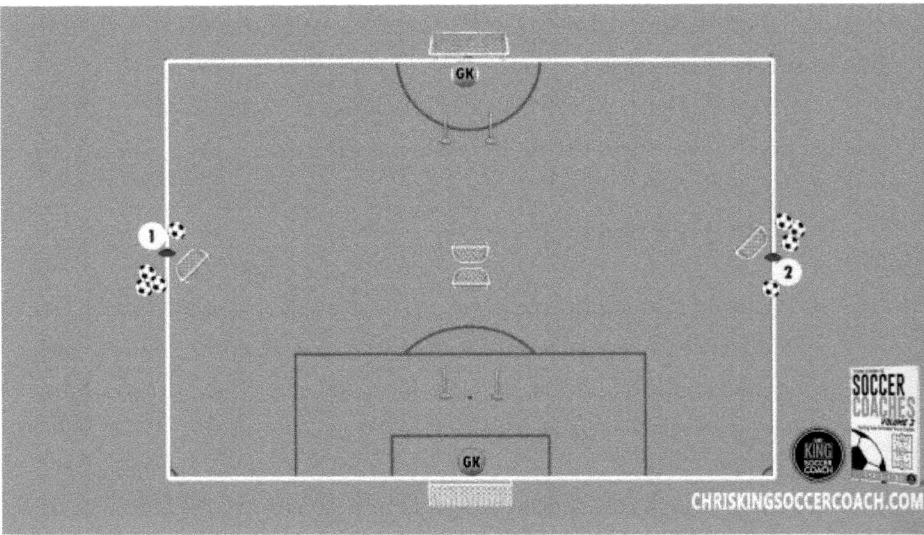

Yellow/Light #1 is putting crosses into the top goalkeeper while at the same time Yellow/Light #2 is putting crosses into the bottom goalkeeper.

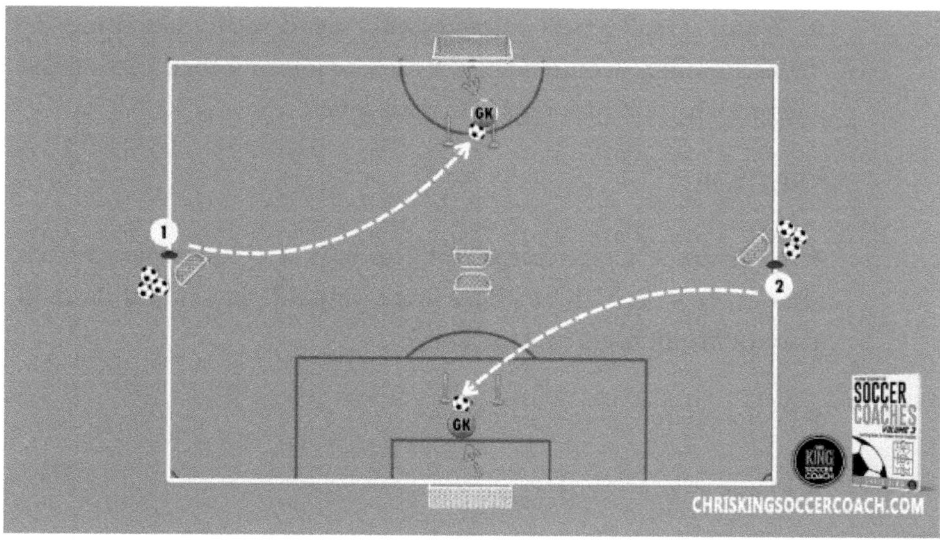

Once the goalkeepers come out and catch the ball they practise quick distribution by throwing the ball into one of the two mini goals or back to the Yellow/Light player.

SESSION 5 "ESSENTIAL SKILLS FOR GOALKEEPERS" DRILL B (THE DEVELOPMENT PHASE) "IMPROVE GOALKEEPERS FOOT SKILLS AND DECISION MAKING"

⟐ PURPOSE:

- To improve the goalkeepers decision making and confidence under pressure when receiving back passes and playing out from the back.

- Pep Guadiloa says that the goalkeeper is the first line of the attack, so try and involve your keeper as much as you can. This drill helps build trust for the goalkeeper to start attacks and improves their foot skills.

- **Note:** Goalkeepers should still spend time practising by themselves, like an outfield player does, to improve their passing and juggling which in turn improves their touch.

◈ **SET UP:**

- **8 Players + 1 Goalkeeper (if you have 2 Goalkeepers switch after every 5 plays. If you have extra outfield players add them in as extra Midfielders or Attackers)**

- ⅓ of a pitch

- 1 large goal

◈ **THE DRILL:**

⅓ of a pitch with a large goal and goalkeeper at one end.

Play 3 Defenders (plus 1 Midfielder waiting to receive the final pass) v 2 Attackers plus 1 Goalkeeper.

2 players start as left and right full backs. Midfield players start 20 yards out from the 18 yard box.

The Attackers start on the cones either side of the midfielders, ready to go in pairs to put pressure on the goalkeeper and Defenders.

To start the play the midfielder dribbles towards their goal and passes back to the goalkeeper. As soon as the pass is made the 2 Attackers can start to press to try to win possession and score.

The goalkeeper, 2 Defenders and 1 Midfielder must now combine to play it back out to the other waiting Midfielder.

Once a pass is made back to the midfielder, a goal is scored or the ball goes out, all players quickly reset and the next group of players start.

◈ **COACHES NOTES:**

- Make sure the goalkeeper has a maximum of 2 touches - we don't want them trying to dribble out of the penalty area or trying step overs! Their first touch should be away from the nearest Attacker and in the direction of where they want their pass to go.

● The Defenders should use the goalkeeper as if they are a regular outfield player. The more they can use the goalkeeper the more confidence they will have in each other.

● The goalkeeper should drop off deeper if a full back has the ball. This way they have created angles so that they can be passed to if required.

☑ **PROGRESSION:**

● Set up for a goal kick and practice playing out.

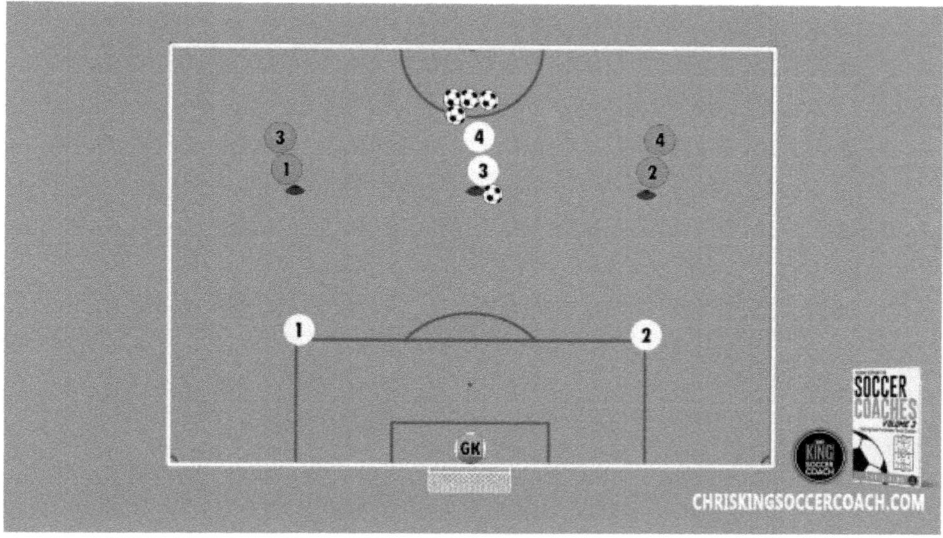

3 Yellow/Light Defenders v 2 Red/Dark Attackers.

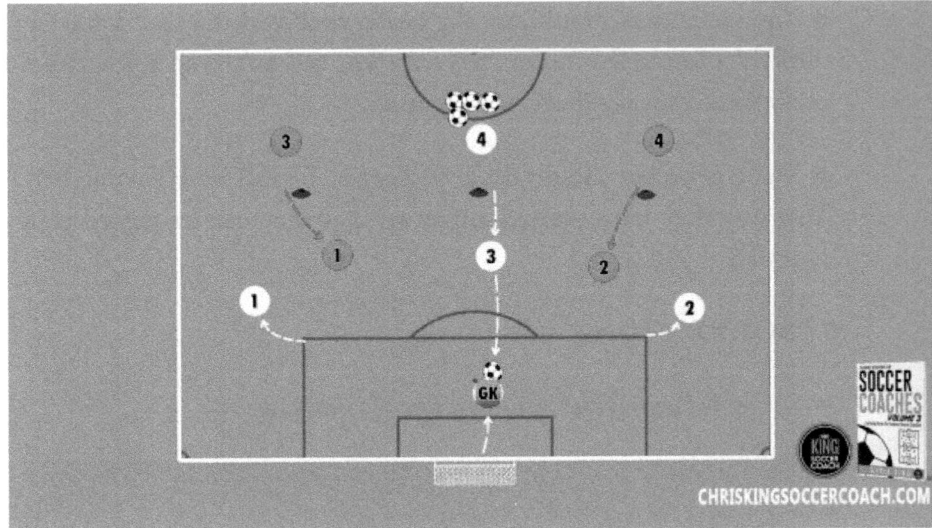

Yellow/Light #3 starts the play by dribbling towards their goal and passing back to their goalkeeper. As soon as the pass is made, play is live. The two Reds/Dark press and try to win the ball and score. The 3 Yellows/Light spread out and aim to play the ball out from the back and get it to their teammate on the cone (Yellow/Light #4). Patience and composure under pressure is key.

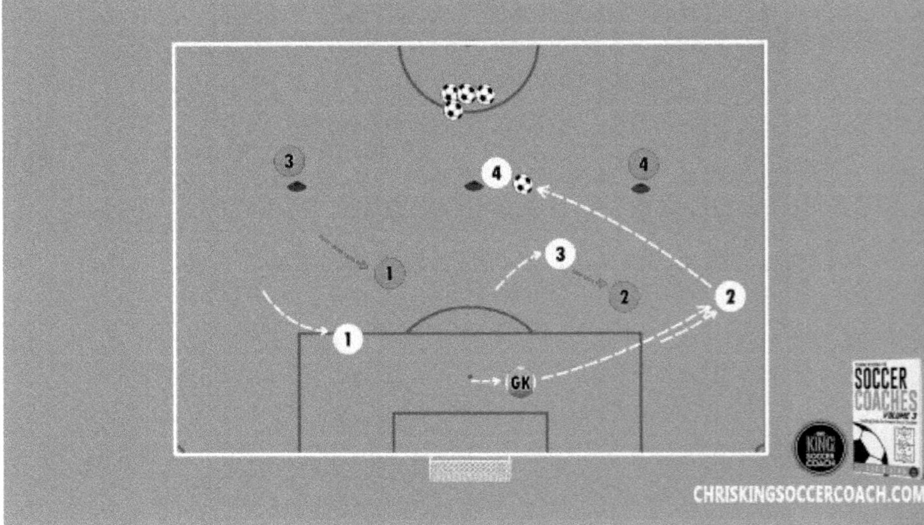

Here the goalkeeper plays it out wide to Yellow/Light #2. Red/Dark were too slow to move across and block the passing lanes so Yellow #2 makes a simple pass to their waiting midfielder (Yellow #4) on the cone.

SESSION 5 "ESSENTIAL SKILLS FOR GOALKEEPERS"
DRILL C (THE GAME PHASE)
"IMPROVING THE GOALKEEPERS CATCHING, DISTRIBUTION AND SHOT STOPPING"

◈ PURPOSE:

- To put the goalkeeper under pressure when coming for crosses and to work on their distribution and shot stopping.

◈ SET UP:

- **8 Players + 2 Goalkeepers**
- ⅓ of a pitch
- 2 large goals

◈ THE DRILL:

Set up a ⅓ of a pitch.

A large goal at each end with a goalkeeper.

2 channels down the sides with 1 winger in each channel who plays on the team in possession. 8 players in the middle section (4v4).

The goalkeepers start the play and can either throw it out to a winger or roll it out to a team mate so they can practise playing out from the back.

◈ COACHES NOTES:

- Everything should be done at pace - just because the wingers don't have an opponent doesn't mean they should slow down. They should have a touch or two to control the ball, settle and then whip the cross in for the striker to attack. Make sure they are delivering most of the crosses in the air because we want to give the goalkeeper practice and gain confidence in coming for the high ball.

- Goalkeepers should be calling "Goalkeepers!" when they come for the ball. In a game, this lets the Defenders know that their goalkeeper is coming to claim the ball. If the goalkeeper can't reach the ball they usually call "Away!" which lets the Defenders know to clear the ball.

- Once the goalkeeper makes the initial catch (or save from a shot) they should be reacting quickly to recover and distribute the ball.

- Encourage the goalkeepers to play it out from the back and not to worry about any mistakes they may make. This is where they get to practise and improve.

☑ **PROGRESSION:**

- Put a time restriction on each play. For example, when a team has possession they have 20 seconds to score. This will help speed up their decision making and intensity.

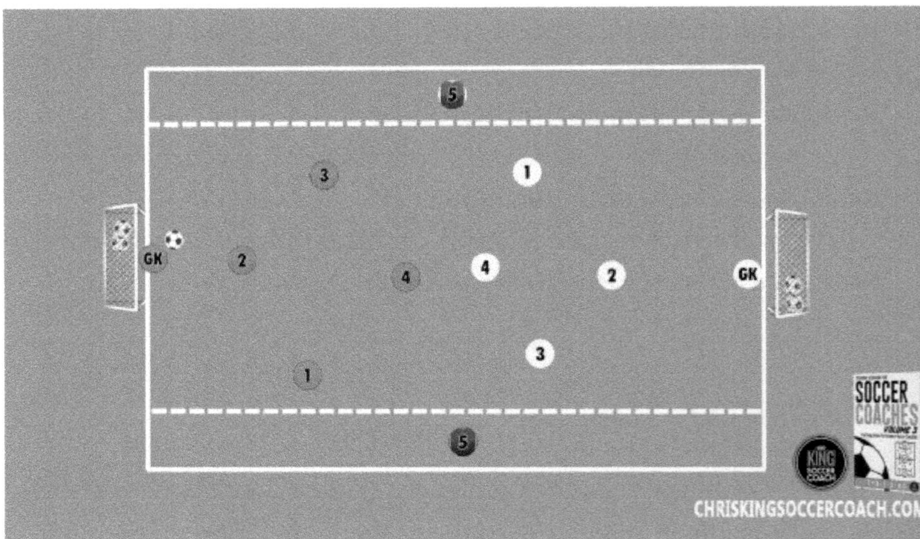

4v4 plus Jokers in the channels playing on whichever team is in possession.

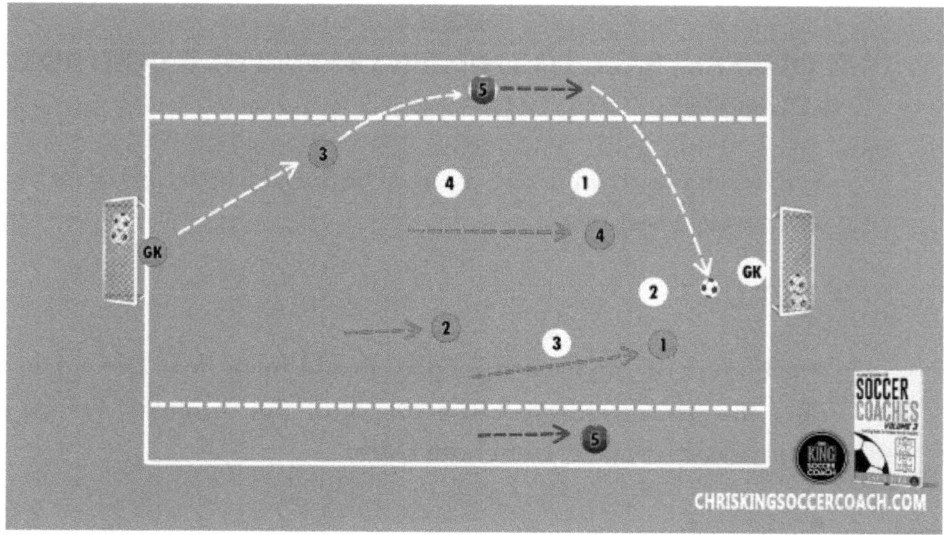

The goalkeeper plays it out to their centre back (Red/Dark #3) who plays it out wide to the winger. Reds/Dark can push forward and get numbers into the danger area. Here the Joker (#5) crosses the ball across the front of the goal. Red/Dark #1 is coming in to attack it at the back post. The other winger pushes forward as well in case the ball comes all the way through.

SESSION 6: ATTACKING CORNER VARIATIONS

<u>Session objective:</u>

Amateur teams don't have hours and hours to work on set plays. But by adding these 3 corner plays to the teams repertoire, they greatly improve their chances of scoring off a corner during the season.

SESSION 6 "ATTACKING CORNER VARIATIONS"

DRILL A
"CORNERS - BALL TO THE CENTRE OF THE 6 YARD BOX "

⟐ PURPOSE:

- To teach players which positions to be in and which runs to make on an attacking corner.

⟐ SET UP:

- **8 Players (if you have more players add them in as Defenders once the Attackers have had a couple of run throughs. Or use them as corner takers from both sides).**

- ⅓ of a pitch

- 1 large goal

⟐ THE DRILL:

Set up players as per the positions in the image for this corner.

An inswinging cross comes in from the corner taker (#1) - practice from both sides. **The delivery should be with pace, at head height and aimed at the centre area, in between the 6 yard box and penalty spot.**

Key Points and positions:

- **4 Attackers (#'s 2,3,4,5) line up in a huddle, starting at the edge of the D.** They will all make runs to set areas inside the 18 yard box to Attack the cross.

- **#2** a direct run to the front post on the 6 yard box.

- **#3** a curved run out and to the back post just outside the 6 yard box. **#4** a curved run to a slightly deeper area behind #3 in case there is a deep ball or a deflection over everybody.

- **#5** a direct run to the centre of the goal just outside the 6 yard box.

- **Player #6 starts on the penalty spot** and makes a run towards the corner taker to outside the 6 yard box (to take a Defender with them and make space inside the danger area. Also if the corner drops short they can flick it on with their head).

- **Player #7 starts on the edge of the box closest to the corner taker.** They make a run towards the corner taker to offer support and hopefully take a Defender out from the box. They also turn and face the goal once the corner is taken and react to any clearances.

- **Player #8 starts outside the box and moves to the top of the box** for any clearances or rebounds.

⯑ COACHES NOTES:

● Make sure all the players know their role. Tell them what their role is and then ask them to repeat back where they are starting and finishing their run.

● Make sure the players attack the cross (and any rebounds and clearances). Be on the move and time the runs to arrive as the ball arrives, don't just jog into position.

● Make sure the crosser focusses on good delivery. If the cross is a floating, slow ball or not in the right spot it mucks everything up for the team. Whip it in around the 6 yard box at head height and give the teammates the best chance to score.

☑ PROGRESSION:

● The corner taker does a short one two pass with the player (#7) who has come to support from the edge of the box. They then cross it to the same spot but they are further out from the touchline so it has changed the angle. Attacking players will have to adjust the timing of their runs (go slightly later or zig zag a bit).

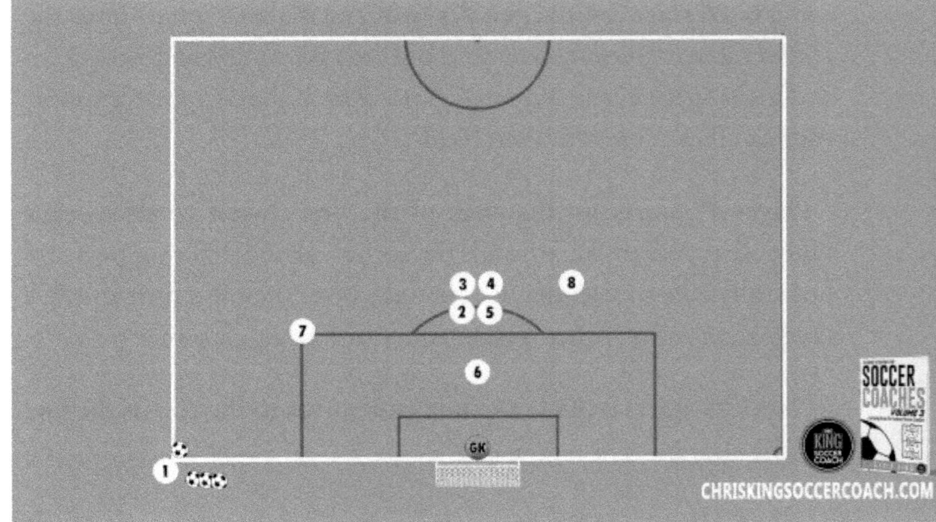

#2,#3,#4 and #5 start together on the edge of the D. #6 starts on the penalty spot and #7 and #8 start around the box.

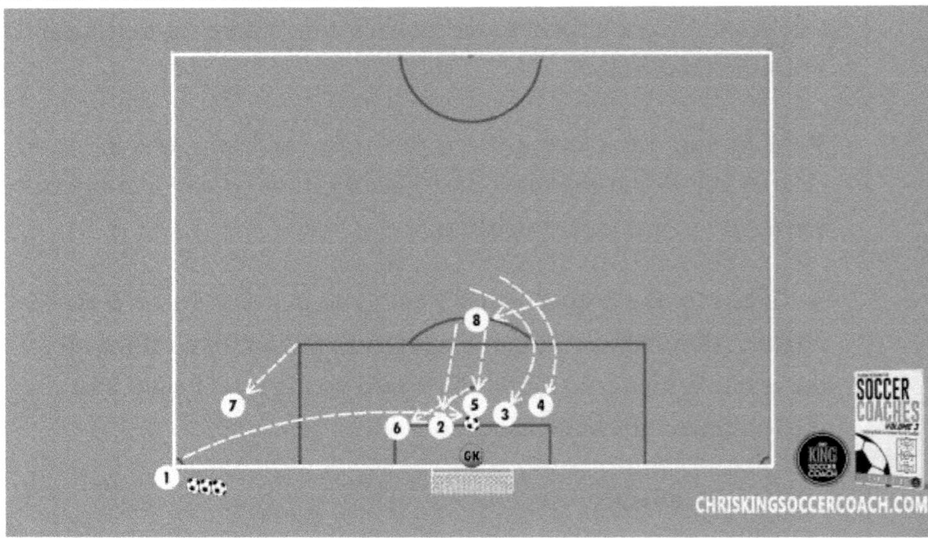

#6 makes a run to the front of the 6 yard box to hopefully take a defender with them. The 4 players from the top of the box make runs to set positions around the 6 yard box to attack the ball that is being delivered to the centre of the 6 yard box. #7 makes a run towards the corner taker to either take a defender with them or to use an alternate play (a one two with #1). #8 stays at the top of the box in case the ball is cleared.

SESSION 6 "ATTACKING CORNER VARIATIONS"
DRILL B
"CORNERS - BALLS TO THE BACK OF THE 6 YARD BOX "

◈ PURPOSE:

- To teach your players which runs to make on an attacking corner.

◈ SET UP:

- **8 Players (if you have more players add them in as Defenders once the Attackers know their runs. Or use them as corner takers from both sides).**

- ⅓ of a pitch

- 1 large goal

◈ THE DRILL:

Set up players as per the positions in the image for this corner.

An inswinging cross from the corner taker (practice from both sides). **The delivery should be with pace, at head height and aimed at the back of the 6 yard box.**

Key Points and positions:

- **4 Attackers (#'s 2,3,4,5) line up in an arc around the D.** 3 players will all make curved runs out the back of the penalty area and back into set positions inside the 6 yard box (#3 inline with the penalty spot, #4 inline with the back post, #5 a bit deeper behind #4). 1 player (#2) will make a straight run to the front of the 6 yard box.

- **Player #6 starts on the edge of the 6 yard box nearest the corner taker** and makes a run towards the corner taker to the edge of the penalty area (to take a defender with them and make space inside the danger area).

- **Player #7 starts near the edge of the box closest to the corner taker.** They make a run towards the corner taker to offer support and hopefully take a defender out from the box. They also turn and face the goal once the corner is taken and react to any clearances.

- **Player #8 holds at the top of the box** for any clearances or rebounds.

⟐ COACHES NOTES:

• Make sure all the players know their role. Tell them what their role is and then ask them to repeat back where they are starting and finishing their run.

• Make sure the players attack the cross (and any rebounds and clearances). Be on the move and time the runs to arrive as the ball arrives, don't just jog into position.

• Make sure the crosser focusses on good delivery. If the ball in is a floating, slow ball or not in the right spot it mucks everything up for the team. Whip it to the back of the 6 yard box. **The cross will have to have some height and curl on it to keep it away from the goalkeeper.**

☑ PROGRESSION:

• The corner taker does a short one two pass to the player who has come to support from the edge of the box (#7). They then cross it to the same spot but it has changed the angle. Attacking players will have to adjust the timing of their runs (go slightly later or zig zag a bit).

• The corner take does a short pass to #6 who has made a run towards them. #6 can now either turn with the ball and take on a Defender, pass the ball across goal or cut it back.

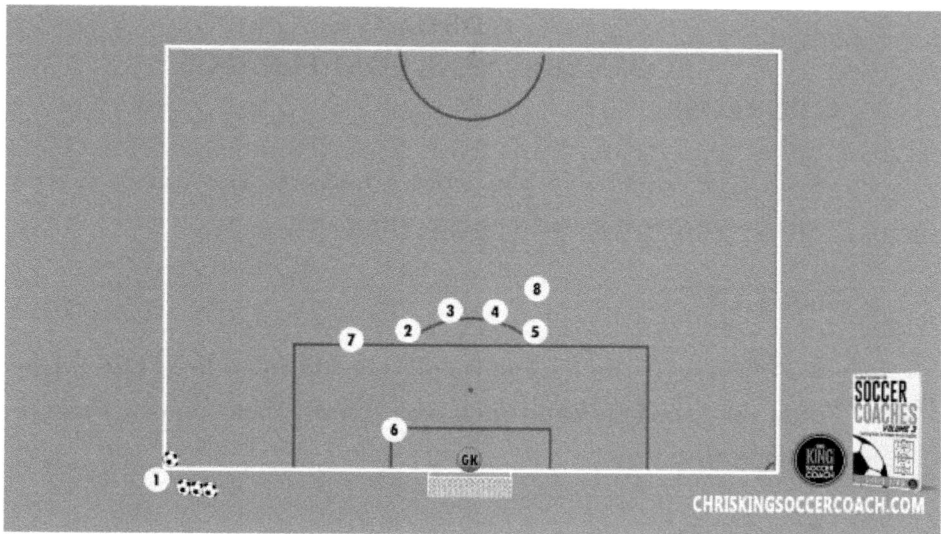

#2,#3,#4 and #5 start together around the edge of the D. #6 starts on the corner of the 6 yard box and #7 and #8 start outside the box.

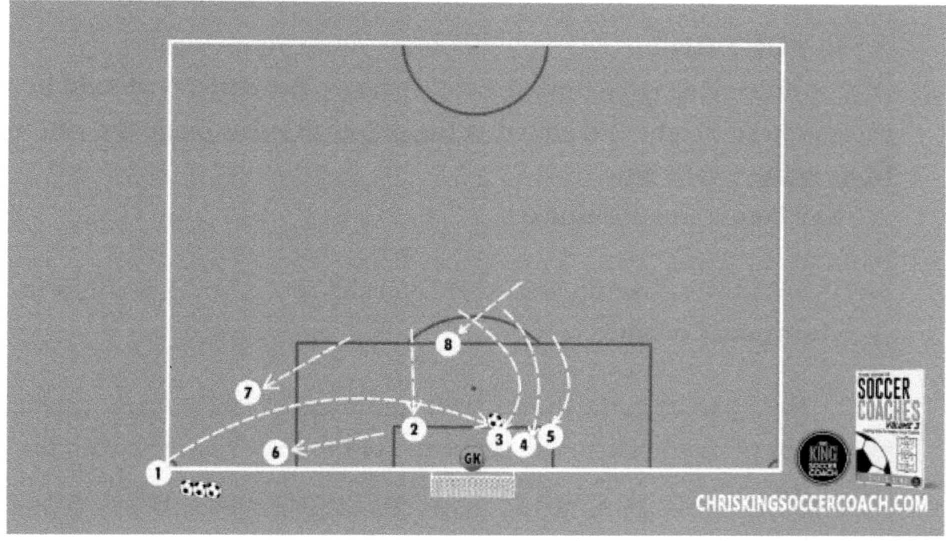

#6 makes a run towards the corner taker to hopefully take a defender with them or for the short pass. The 4 players from the top of the box make runs to set positions around the 6 yard box to attack the ball that is being delivered to the back post. #7 makes a run towards the corner taker to either take a defender with them or to use an alternate play (see progression). #8 stays at the top of the box in case the ball is cleared.

SESSION 6 "ATTACKING CORNER VARIATIONS"

DRILL C
"CORNERS - NEAR POST FLICK ON"

◈ **PURPOSE:**

- To add variation to your corner routines. This can be a very effective corner and catch the opposition out.

◈ **SET UP:**

- **8 Players (if you have more players add them in as Defenders once the Attackers know their runs. Or use them as corner takers from both sides).**

- ⅓ of a pitch

- 1 large goal

◈ **THE DRILL:**

An inswinging cross from the corner taker. **The delivery should be with pace, at head height and <u>aimed at the player that has made the run to the front of the 6 yard box</u>.**

Key Points and positions:

- 5 Attackers line up around the penalty spot (#'s 2,3,4,5,6): 3 in front and 2 behind.

- The 3 players in the front starting positions are: #2 in line with the front post; #3 in line with the centre of the goal; #4 in line with the back post.

- Players #5 and #6 line up behind players #3 and #4.

- Players #7 and #8 line up on the edge of the box.

In Play:

- **The corner taker (#1) plays it in the air to the front corner** of the 6 yard box.

- **Player #2 makes a run to the front of the 6 yard box** to flick on the cross to the back post.

- **Player #3 makes a run to the centre edge of the 6 yard box.**

- **Player #4 makes a run to the back of the 6 yard box.**

- **Player #5 makes a run to the area between the penalty spot and 6 yard box.**

- **Player #6 makes a run to the same area but in line with the back post**

- **Player #7 stays around the edge of the box** for any rebounds or clearances.

- **Player #8 makes a run to the front of the box** to hopefully drag a defender out.

◈ COACHES NOTES:

- The flick changes the height and angle of the cross so it makes it hard for the goalkeeper to pick up the flight of the ball.

- It is somewhat random what happens after the flick on. But it is so close to the goal that there is a good chance that if any Attacking player gets a touch on it, it will end up in the goal.

- Make sure all the players know their role. Tell them what their role is and then ask them to repeat back where they are starting and finishing their run.

- The player that makes the flick on is key here - they need to time their run to get to the edge of the 6 yard box just as the ball arrives.

The flick should come off the top of their head and loop to the back post area. The goalkeeper and Defenders will be drawn to the front post where it looks like the ball is coming to. But instead it will be flicked to the back post where there aren't as many Defenders or the goalkeeper.

● Players should be on the move and time their runs to arrive as the ball does, don't just jog into position.

● Make sure the crosser focusses on good delivery. Whip it to the player at the front of the 6 yard box.

☑ **PROGRESSION:**

● The corner taker passes the ball to Player #2. They can either pass back to the corner taker who does a deep cross to the back post. Or if you've got a skilled, confident player, they can quickly turn and take on their Defender or pass it inside to a teammate.

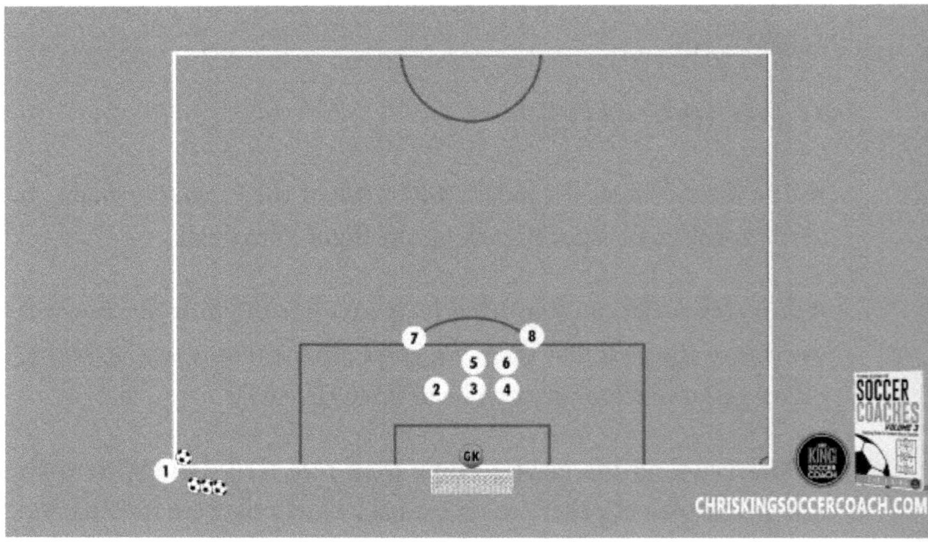

#2,#3,#4,#5 and #6 start together around the penalty area. #7 and #8 start at the edge of the box on the D.

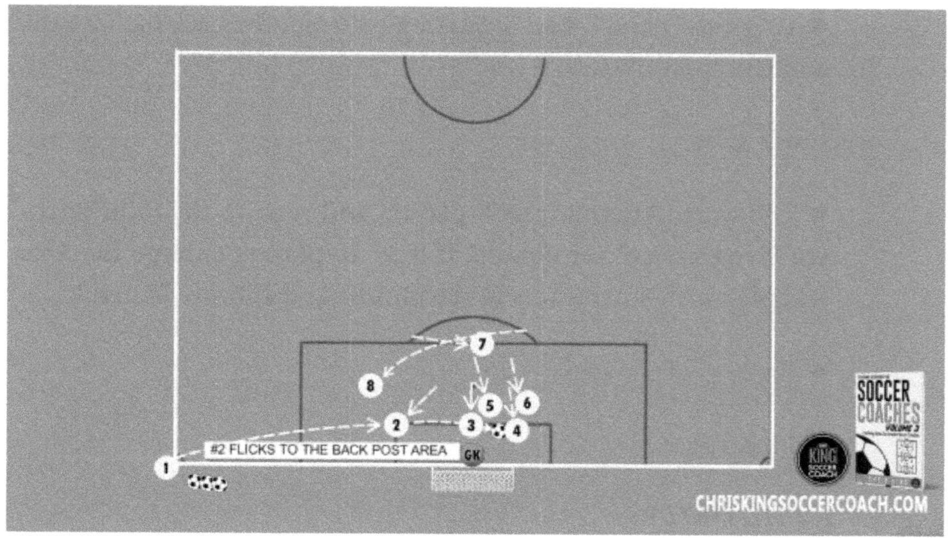

#2 runs to the front of the 6 yard box to flick on the cross. #3,#4,#5 and #6 attack the area around the back post where the flick on should go. #7 stays at the top of the box for any clearances. #8 makes a run to the front post to take a Defender away.

SESSION 7: PLAYING OUT FROM THE BACK

Session Objective:

Giving players confidence to play out from the back.

SESSION 7 "A"

DRILL A (THE LEARNING PHASE)

"BACK 4 RONDO "

� PURPOSE:

- To get the back 4 used to playing out from the backline into the midfield and forwards.

◈ SET UP:

- **7 Players (Alternatively 8 players and remove the mini goal - see 'Progression' for details. If 9 or 10 players enlarge the area and play with 3 Attackers in the middle and another Defender)**

- 30x20 yard rectangle

- 1 mini goal

◈ THE DRILL:

Set up a 30x20 yard rectangle.

5 Defenders v 2 Attackers.

Set up in the shape of a back 4 and a Defensive midfielder:

1 Defender inside the square. 2 Defenders on the back line and 1 Defender on each of the two sides.

2 Attackers inside the square.

1 mini goal on the top line.

Defenders aim to pass the ball sideways until an option opens up to pass to their teammate in the middle who in turn passes into the mini goal. Alternatively, one of the Defenders on the side can pass directly into the mini goal.

The mini goal represents, in a real game situation, being able to pass forward into an Attacking midfielder or forward.

Once the Attackers have won possession 5 times swap roles.

Note: The Defender in the square represents a Defensive midfielder and the goal represents a more attacking midfielder. During a game, play will usually build up through these players. The Defensive midfielder will be working fairly hard so swap them out regularly.

◈ COACHES NOTES:

- Body shape and passing to the teammates back foot is key here. We want to be able to move the ball forward as soon as the opportunity arises. So players should be facing forward when they receive the ball. And they should take it on their back foot whenever possible to play forward.

• The Defender in the middle should be dropping in and out of space, finding a yard or two to receive a pass from one of the back four. If they can, they should take the ball on the turn or facing forward so they can pass into the mini goal. If they can't pass forward a quick one-two with a teammate will drag an Attacker with them and will open space up for a teammate.

☑ **PROGRESSION:**

• If you have an extra player, replace the goal with that player. And then play can be continuous, going from one end to the other.

• When the Attackers in the middle win possession, another Defender drops into the square to make it 2v2 and play until the Defenders win back possession. This teaches players to press as soon as they lose possession and try to win the ball back straight away.

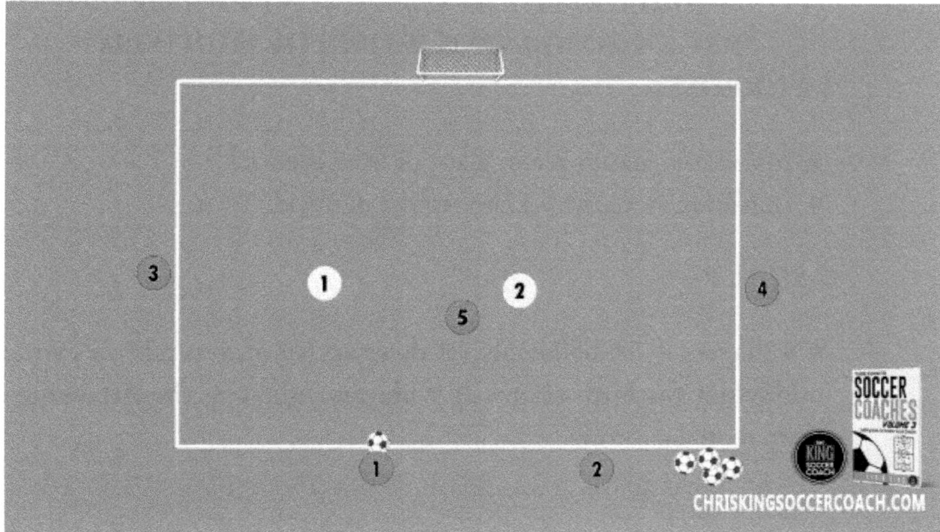

Reds/Dark are in their Defensive shape (2 centre backs, a left and right fullback and 1 Defensive midfield). They look to play the ball around until there is a clear opportunity to get the ball forward into the mini goal either directly from a fullback or through the Defensive midfielder.

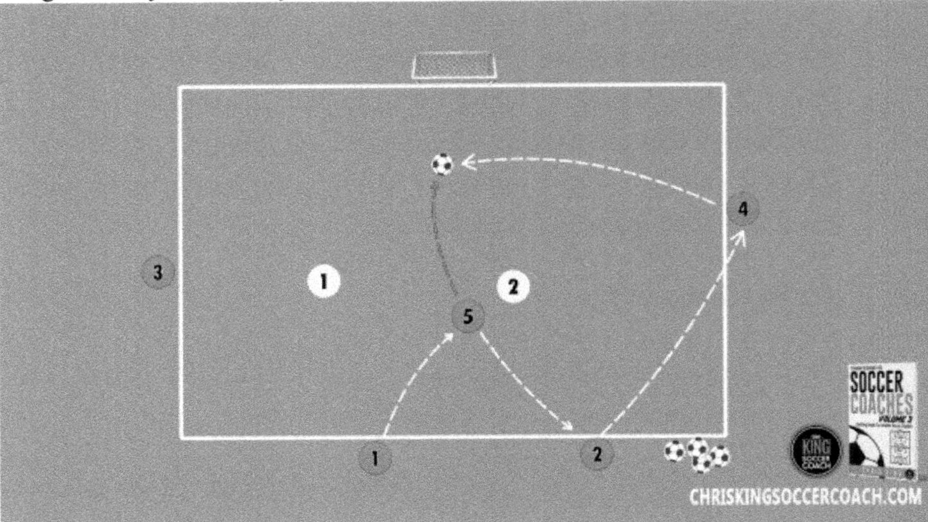

Quick ball movement from the Reds/Dark allows them to get the ball wide and back in behind the Yellow/Light press so that Red/Dark #5 can run on to the ball and pass forward into the goal.

SESSION 7 "PLAYING OUT FROM THE BACK"
DRILL B (THE DEVELOPMENT PHASE)
"BACK 4 COMBINING WITH THE MIDFIELD"

⟐ PURPOSE:

- To develop confidence to play out from the back.
- Transition from the backline to the midfield.

⟐ SET UP:

- **8 Players + 1 Goalkeeper (If there are 10 players add an extra midfielder for both teams. If 9 players, add 1 to the Attacking team to make it 5v4)**

- ⅓ of a pitch

- 1 large goal + 3 mini goals

◈ THE DRILL:

Set up a 40x35 yard area out from the goal. Place 3 mini goals at the far end.

Place soccer balls behind the large goal ready for the goalkeeper to start play.

5 Defenders v 3 Attackers (Defenders playing towards the mini goals, Attackers towards the large goal).

The 2 centre backs are looking to combine with the 2 full backs (the fullbacks should try to get high and wide) and the Defensive midfielder to play it forward. They are aiming to get it to the opposite end and score in the mini goals.

The Attacking team is aiming to win possession and score quickly in the large goal before the Defenders can get their defensive shape back. If they win possession they have 20 seconds to score.

As soon as a goal is scored or the ball goes out, players reset and the goalkeeper plays it out to a centre back.

Play for 5 minutes, rest for 1 minute then restart (or swap team roles).

◈ COACHES NOTES:

- The fullbacks should aim to get high and wide, allowing themselves space to come back in to receive the ball from the centre backs or goalkeeper.

- Passing from the Defenders should be fast but they should use patience before passing into the midfield - if a pass into the midfielder isn't on or there is no space for the full backs to go forward, play it back across goal and come out the other side. This will force the Attacking team to adjust their shape and it will open up other options and angles for a pass.

- The goalkeeper should be organising the back four, constantly talking and telling them their options.

- If you have smart centre backs and a quality defensive midfielder, the centre backs can split and go out wide which allows the

Defensive midfielder to drop in to receive the ball from the goalkeeper. This will add another dimension to playing out as the fullbacks can push even higher. Then the centre backs can push out into the space they have vacated.

☑ PROGRESSION:

- Full backs can be neutral so they play on whichever team has possession.

- If the Attacking team scores, they get to keep possession and restart with a ball from the mini goal end.

- If it's too easy for the Defenders to play out, add in an extra Attacker, make it two touch for the Defenders or make the Defensive midfielder a Joker so they play on whichever team is in possession.

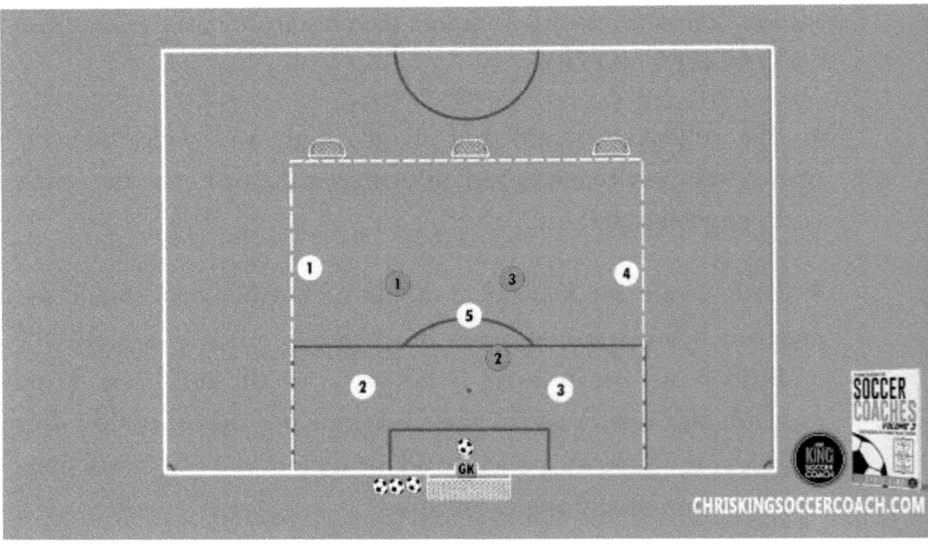

5v3. Play starts from the goalkeeper and Yellows/Light look to play it out from the back and score in the mini goals. If the Reds/Dark win possession they attack the large goal.

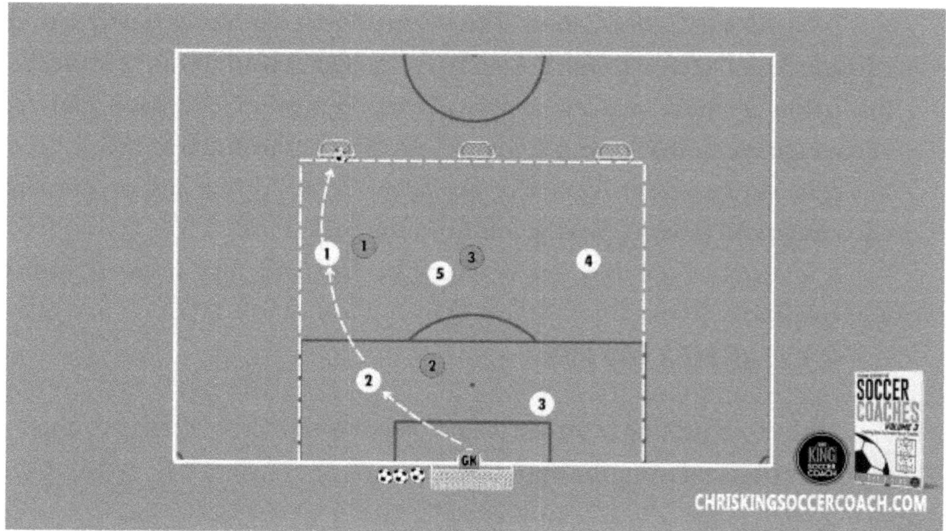

Here the Yellow/Light centre back (#2) passes to the left full back (Yellow/ Light #1) as Red/Dark #1 hasn't shut them down quickly enough.

SESSION 7 "PLAYING OUT FROM THE BACK"
DRILL C (THE GAME PHASE)
"7v7 PLAYING OUT FROM THE BACK "

◈ PURPOSE:

- Improve your team's ability to keep possession and transition into attack by playing out from the back.

◈ SET UP:

- **14 Players + 2 Goalkeepers (can play with any number of players - if less players remove a midfielder and if more players add in strikers)**
- ¾ of a pitch
- 2 large goal

◈ THE DRILL:

Set up a ¾ pitch with large goals at each end.

7v7 with a 4-1-2 formation. This setup is more like a back 4 with a midfield triangle 3 (1 Defensive and 2 Attacking) as opposed to having 2 strikers. This formation is more realistic when playing out from the back and it will encourage the fullbacks to get forward to support the midfielders.

Play always starts from the goalkeepers (no throw ins or corners) to encourage and practise playing out from the back .

If a team scores they get to keep the ball and play restarts from their goalkeeper.

◈ COACHES NOTES:

- Lots of passing from the team in possession. This will help counter any pressing from the opponents.

- Players should adapt an open body shape when receiving the ball so they can play it forward when possible.

- Teammates should be providing options for the player on the ball - they should have a forward, sideways and backwards option to pass to whenever realistically possible.

☑ PROGRESSION:

- Play with no goals. Instead, focus on keeping possession. 10 passes equals a goal or can a team keep the ball for 1 minute (which equals 1 goal)? Sometimes in a game, players think "Score! Score! Score!", whereas keeping possession is just as important. Especially if in a game your team is ahead and you want to just keep possession to see the final minutes out.

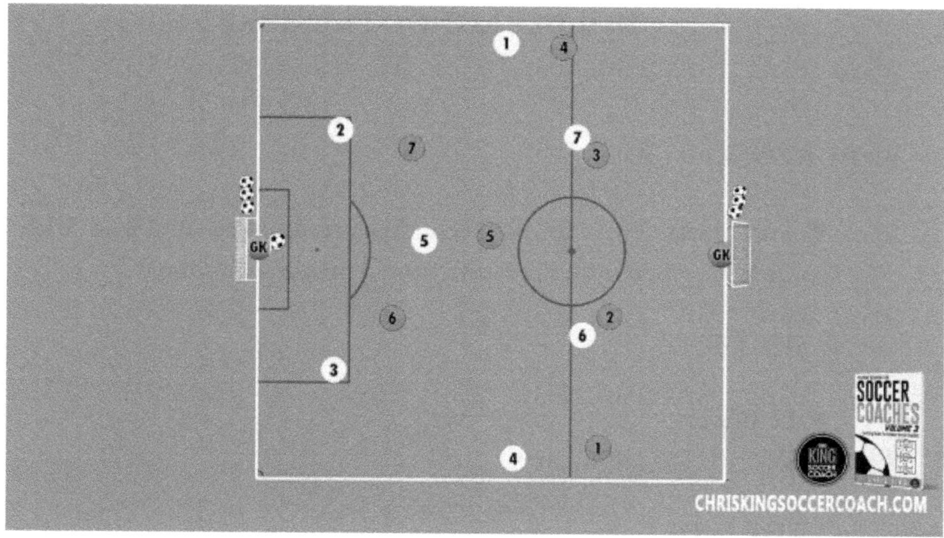

7v7 plus goalkeepers. Play starts from the goalkeepers each time a ball goes out or a goal is scored. The fullbacks look to get high and wide to leave space for the centre backs or for them to come back into.

SESSION 8: DECISION MAKING UNDER PRESSURE

Session Objective:

This session aims to help players keep their composure and gain confidence by putting them in pressure situations.

SESSION 8 "DECISION MAKING UNDER PRESSURE"

DRILL A (THE LEARNING PHASE)

"DOUBLE RONDO PRESSURE "

◈ PURPOSE:

- For players to learn to keep their composure and pass with confidence when under pressure from a pressing opponent.

◈ SET UP:

- **12 Players**
- Two 15x15 yard squares

◈ THE DRILL:

Set up two 15x15 yard squares close to each other.

3 Attackers in each square with a ball.

The 6 Defenders wait 5 yards outside the first square.

As soon as an Attacker makes the first pass, 1 Defender enters the first square to press and either win the ball or knock it out. The Attackers pass until they make 8 passes or they lose possession.

As soon as the Defender wins the ball or knocks it out, or the Attackers make 8 passes, the Defender runs over to the next square and does the same. At the same time a new Defender enters the first square.

Sometimes there will be a slight overlap and there will be 2 Defenders in a square at once. This is fine. The 2 Defenders simply work together to win the ball.

Play for 2 minutes then swap the roles of the team.

◈ COACHES NOTES:

- The Attacking team should spread out to make it hard for the Defender to press.

- Attackers should use one and two touch play to move the ball quickly.

● Play to the teammates' back foot so they can play forward or backwards.

● When pressing, can the Defender read the Attackers movements, body shape or eyes to see where they intend to pass?

- If their hips are closed they may be going to pass back where the ball came from.

- If they are open they may be going to pass forward.

☑ **PROGRESSION:**

● Attackers pass for as long as they can. If they get to 15 passes the Defender does 10 push ups when they finish.

● Make it into a competition: Time both teams, with the Defending team going through 3 times each, and see how long it takes them to finish. Then swap roles and time that team. The fastest team wins.

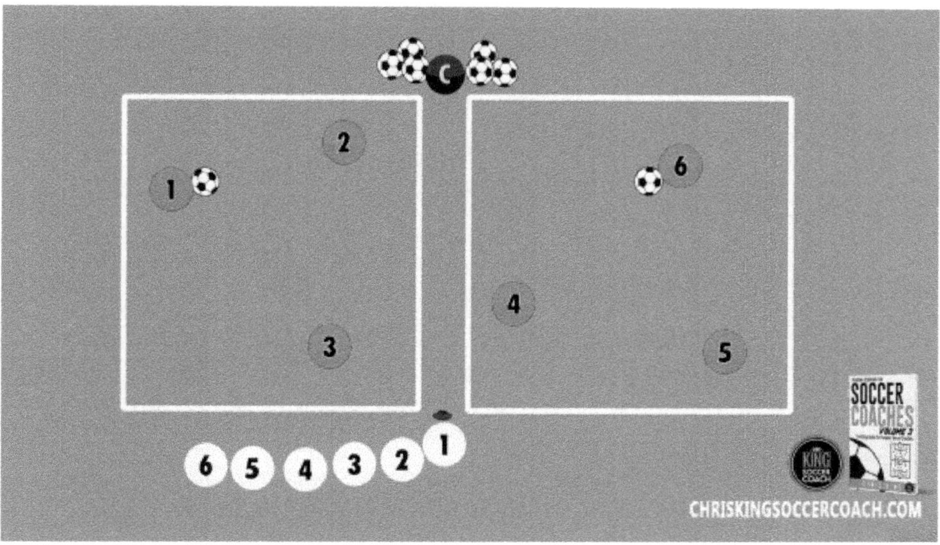

2 rondos are set up side by side. A Defender (Yellow/Light #1) enters the first square and tries to win the ball. As soon as they win the ball (or the Reds/Dark

make 8 passes) they move onto the other square to do the same. The next Yellow/Light starts as soon as the first Yellow/Light moves to the second square.

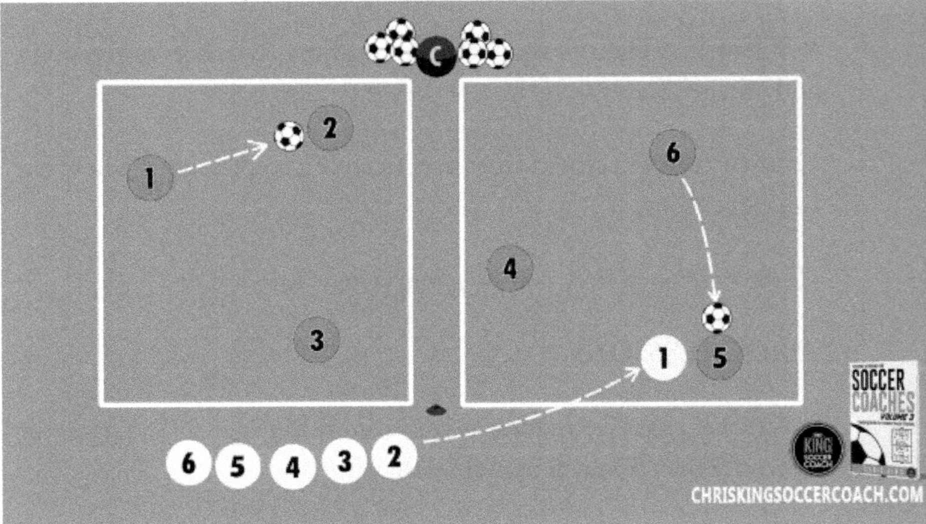

Here Yellow/Light #1 presses Red/Dark #5 straight away.

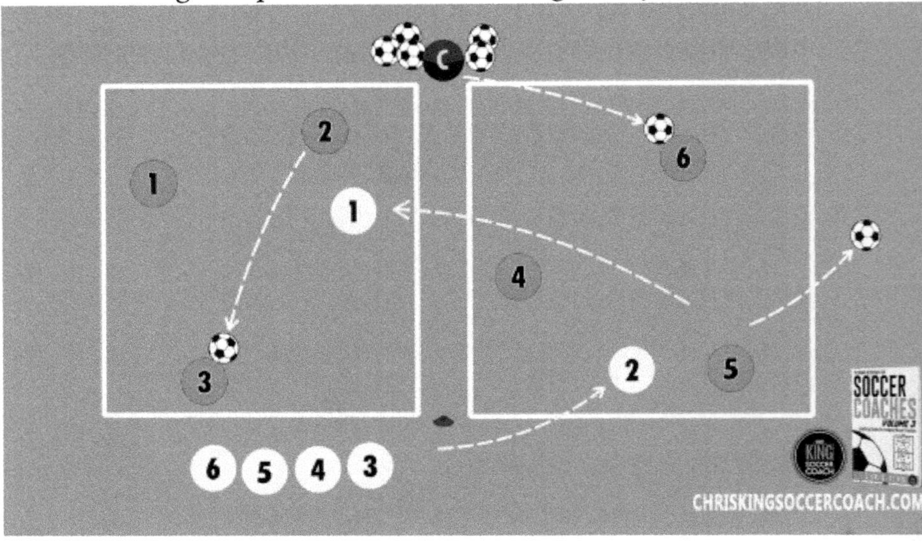

Yellow/Light #1 wins the ball and kicks it out and quickly moves onto the other square. Yellow/Light #2 enters the first square straight away (the coach has passed a new ball into the Reds/Dark).

SESSION 8 "DECISION MAKING UNDER PRESSURE"
DRILL B (THE DEVELOPMENT PHASE)
"3v2 ATTACK v DEFENCE"

◈ PURPOSE:

- To put players in different scenarios around the goal to improve both the Attackers and Defenders decision making.

◈ SET UP:

- **12 Players + 1 Goalkeeper (or use any amount of players - half as Defenders and half as Attackers)**
- 40x25 yard pitch
- 1 large goal + 2 mini goals

◈ THE DRILL:

Set up a large rectangle 40x25 yards split in half.

6 Defenders start behind the goal (3 either side).

6 Attackers start on the line in between the two mini goals.

The goalkeeper starts the play by throwing it out to the 3 Attackers who attack the large goal. 2 Defenders run out as soon as the ball is thrown, getting as high up the pitch as possible to press the Attackers.

The attackers try to score in the large goal, the Defenders try to win possession and score in the mini goals.

Once either happens, or the ball goes out, reset and 2 new Defenders play against 3 new Attackers.

◈ COACHES NOTES:

● Defenders getting out *quickly* and pressing the player on the ball is very important. Keep the Attackers as far from goals as possible.

● Attackers should spread out and move the ball quickly. This makes it hard for the 2 Defenders and also helps create an opening for a shot.

● The goalkeeper should be talking and organising the 2 Defenders.

☑ **PROGRESSION:**

● Enlarge the area and make it 4 Attackers v 3 Defenders (instead of 3v2).

● Make it 3v3 or have the Attackers outnumbered and make it 2 Attackers v 3 Defenders. All of this helps with decision making in different situations.

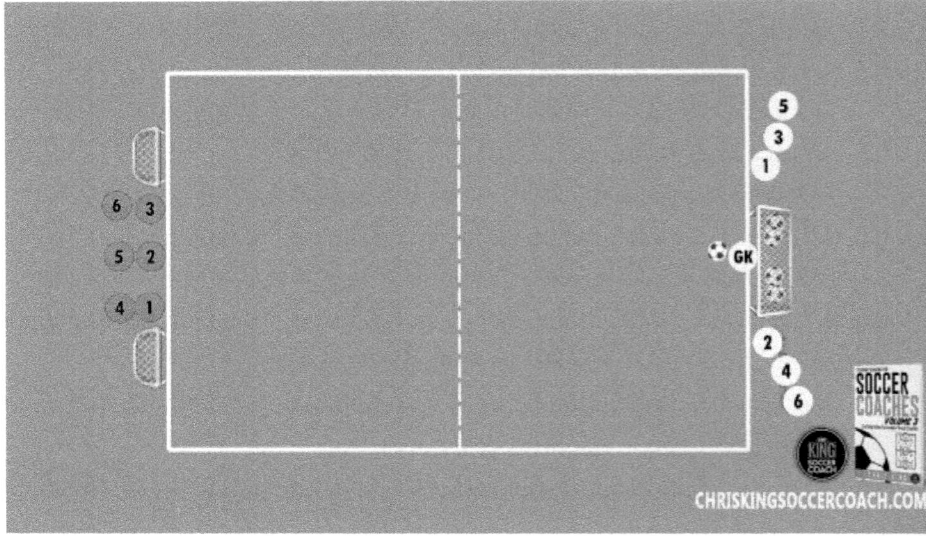

Reds/Dark in groups of 3 attack the large goal to the right. Yellows/Light, in pairs, defend the large goal and try to score in the mini goals if they win possession.

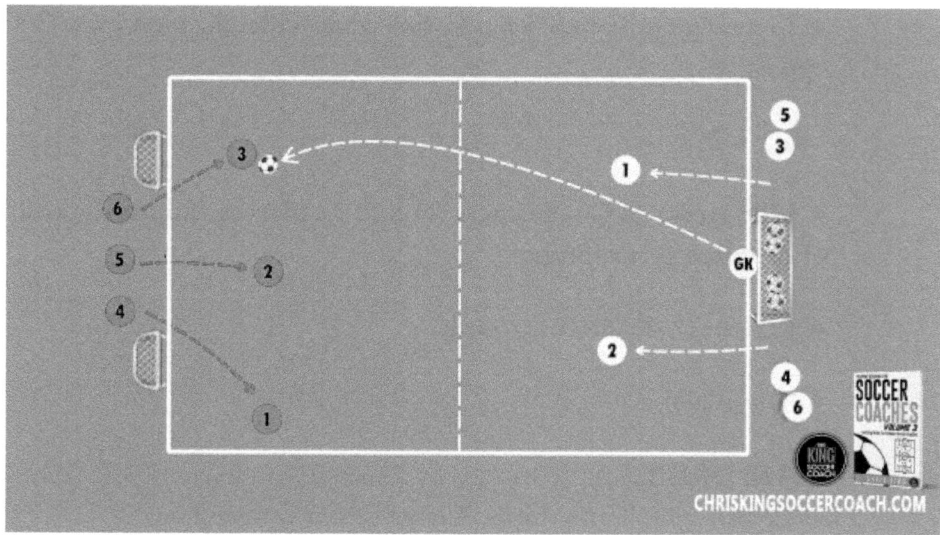

The goalkeeper plays it out to the 3 Reds/Dark and 2 Yellows/Light try and get out to them as quickly as they can.

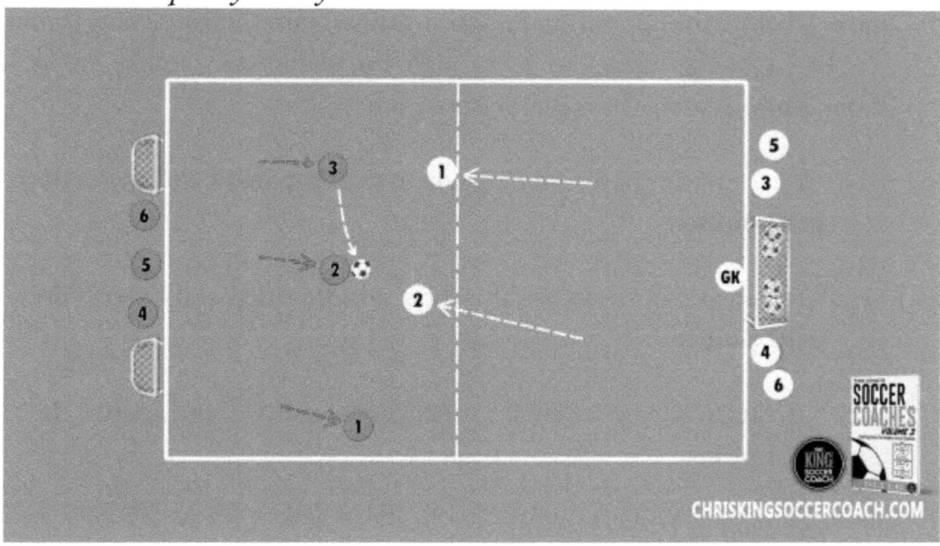

Red/Dark #1 goes out wide to the wing to make the area large and harder for the Yellows/Light to defend. Yellow/Light defend the danger area (where the ball is) and if the ball goes wide to Red/Dark #1 they can move over and adjust.

SESSION 8 "DECISION MAKING UNDER PRESSURE"

DRILL C (THE GAME PHASE)

"6v6 PRESSURE GAME"

◈ PURPOSE:

- To stay composed and keep passing while under the press from the opposition.

◈ **SET UP:**

- **12 Players + 2 Goalkeepers (or 8 to 18 players - adjust the size of the pitch accordingly)**

- 1/2 a pitch divided into thirds

- 2 large goal

◈ **THE DRILL:**

Divide half a pitch into thirds. A large goal at each end.

6v6 with 2 goalkeepers.

The Defending team presses as high up the pitch as they can, trying to win the ball before the opposition can get organised into their attacking formation.

To encourage teams to press high up, points for a goal are awarded depending on where the attack started from:

- If a team wins possession high up in their **top third and score, they get 3 points.**

- If a team wins possession in their **middle third and scores, they get 2 points.**

- If a team wins possession in their **bottom third and scores, they get 1 point.**

First team to 10 points wins.

When a goal is scored, the other team gets possession and play starts from their goalkeeper. The opposition should instantly press as high up as they can. This is so they can try and win possession in their 2 or 3 point zone and get maximum points if they score a goal.

◈ **COACHES NOTES:**

• **KEY PRESSING POINT:** As soon as a team loses possession you want them pressing instantly! You don't want them dropping off back into their bottom thirds. In a game, if a team is attacking and they are near the opposition's goal, chances are they have a decent number of players up there. So if they lose possession, we want these players' instant reaction to be to press together and win the ball high up. If after a few seconds the opposition have passed their way out of the press, then the team can drop back and defend deeper.

• Teammates should be pressing and moving together. There is no use just one or two players pressing and the other teammates sitting off. For example, if there is a winger out wide waiting to receive the ball but the team loses possession on the opposite wing, they should instantly move over to join in the press to help their teammates (making it a compact press). The winger shouldn't stay over the far side and let the opposition pass their way out using a player that the winger could've been pressing.

• The team in possession should try and stay composed and pass their way around or through the press. Use the goalkeeper and keep the ball moving so the opposition have to adjust. This drill is for players to get used to passing under pressure, so encourage them to keep passing even if they get caught on the ball or passes go astray.

☑ **PROGRESSION:**

• Remove the thirds and let the players play without restrictions and see if they still press high.

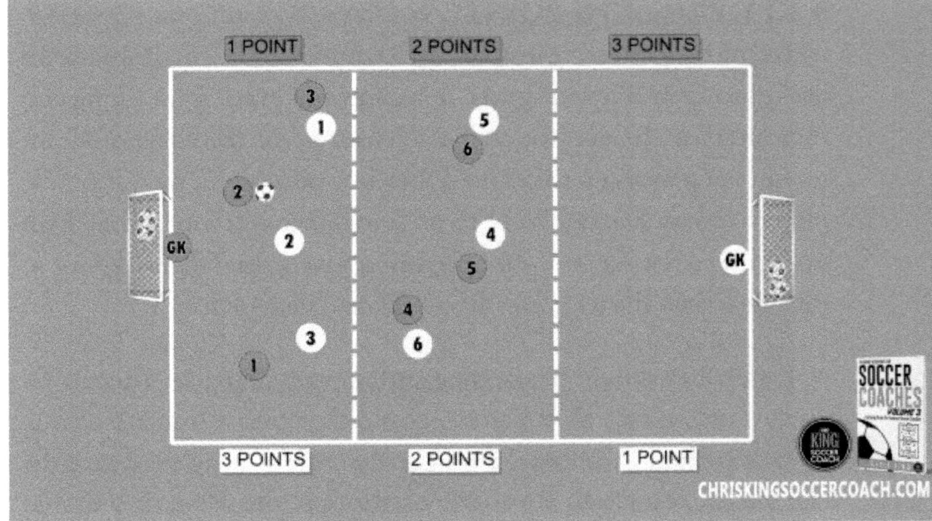

Here Red/Dark is trying to play it out from the back. Yellow/Light have pressed up into the top two thirds to reduce the space which makes it hard for the Reds/Dark to pass their way out.

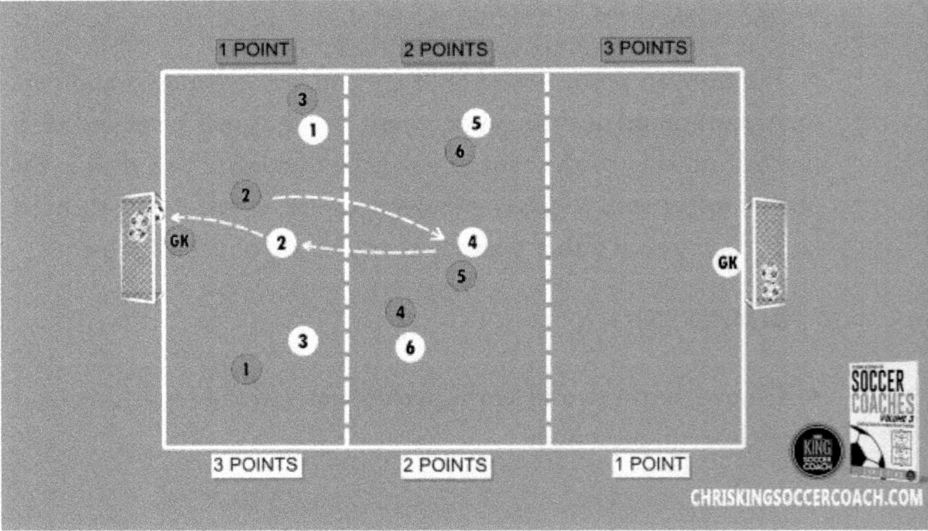

In this scenario, Red/Dark #2 has tried to pass to Red/Dark #5 but Yellow/Light #4 has read the pass. They intercept, pass to their teammate (Yellow/Light #2) who scores. The Yellow/Light team receive 2 points because they won possession in the 2 point zone.

SESSION 9: TRANSITION PLAY

Session Objective:

To improve the team's ability to keep possession and transition from the backline, into midfield and into attack.

Also to achieve a playing tempo.

SESSION 9 "TRANSITION PLAY"

DRILL A (THE DEVELOPMENT PHASE)

"5v2 RONDO "

PURPOSE:

- Improve the players ability to retain possession and play forward to transition into attack.

SET UP:

- **7 Players (or if 8 players add in another Attacking midfielder)**
- 25x15 yard rectangle
- 4 mannequins (or poles)

THE DRILL:

Set up a 25x15 yard rectangle with 4 mannequins (or poles) in the centre of the rectangle a few yards apart.

4 Attacking players on each side of the rectangle. 1 Attacking player in the middle and 2 Defenders in the middle.

The Attackers aim to move the ball from one end to the other.

The central Attacker must touch the ball at least once in the transition from one end to the other.

If the 2 Defenders win the ball, they swap with 2 outside players.

If the ball hits the mannequins, play on - this helps with players' reactions.

The coach should feed the players on the end balls so it is non stop.

A goal is scored by the team in possession either making 10 consecutive passes or by transferring the ball to one end and back again.

◈ COACHES NOTES:

- When this drill is in full flow it's great to watch. **Don't expect the players to be perfect straight away. But definitely persist with this drill and use it where possible.** It greatly improves players speed of thought, touch, movement, support of the ball carrier and angled passing.

- Attackers must constantly be offering support to the player on the ball, moving up and down the sides and the middle.

- Instead of passing directly sideways, look to do second and third line passing when possible (second line passing: to the side but forward. Third line passing: through the middle splitting two defenders).

- Move the ball with short one and two touch passing which inturn moves the Defenders and opens up different passing angles.

- If the players are more advanced and skillful, see if they can get a tempo and rhythm going.

☑ PROGRESSION:

- Make it one touch. This will make teammates support the player on the ball. And the player on the ball will improve their awareness of where to pass and to think ahead of time where they can pass before receiving the ball.

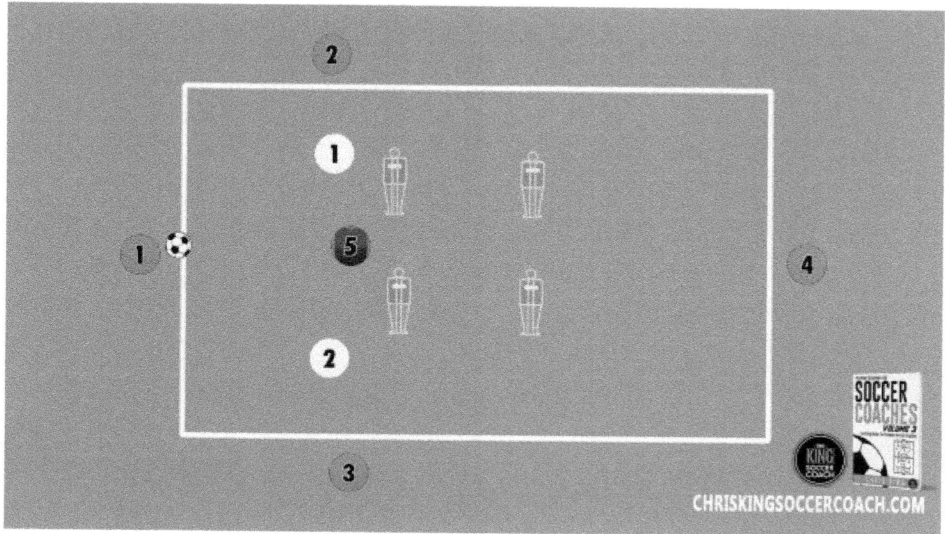

4 Reds/Dark combine with the Blue/Darker #5 to transition the ball from end to end.

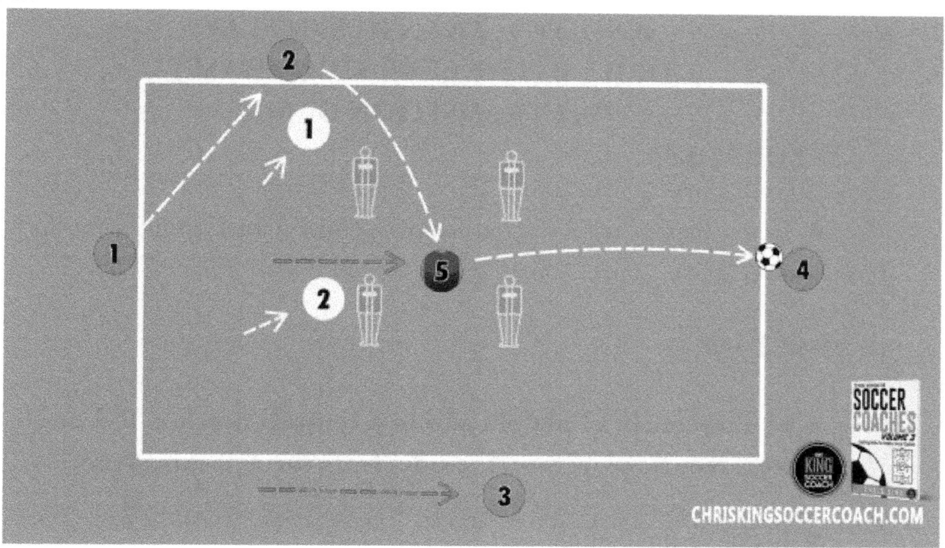

The ball must go through the middle player (Blue/Darker #5). Here Red/Dark have successfully transitioned the ball to the outside, back to the middle and to the end player.

If Red/Dark can transition the ball back to the other end they receive 1 point (or alternatively, if they complete 10 passes they also receive a point).

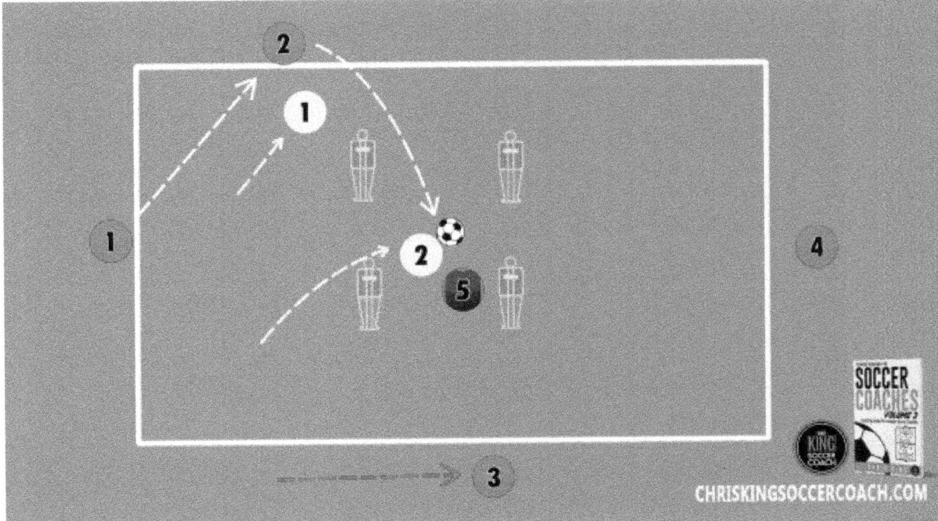

Yellow/Light #2 intercepts the pass and wins the ball. So the Yellow/Light Defenders swap roles with two Reds/Dark players.

SESSION 9 "TRANSITION PLAY"
DRILL B (THE LEARNING PHASE)
"7v4 TRANSITION GAME"

◈ PURPOSE:

- To get players used to transitioning from Attack to Defence and visa versa.

◈ SET UP:

- **11 Players (If 12 players add in a central Attacker. If 9 or 10 players remove players on the sides from the Attacking team)**
- 30x20 yard rectangle

◈ THE DRILL:

Set up a 30x20 yard rectangle.

4 Defenders start inside the rectangle.

6 Attackers are placed around the square (1 at each end and 2 on each side) plus 1 Attacker inside the rectangle.

The Attacking team aims to work the ball from end to end, using the outside players and the central Attacking player (**the central player must touch the ball at least once** as the ball transitions to the other end).

This shape mirrors a team working the ball out from the backline, to the midfield (or out wide) and to the forward line.

Defenders try to win the ball (they must stay within the rectangle). When they have won possession 3 times they swap roles with 4 Attackers.

Every 3 minutes swap the central Attacker.

⯑ COACHES NOTES:

- It is fairly intense play, so have a 30 second rest every 5 minutes. During this short break, talk about things such as tempo of play for the Attackers and working as a team for the Defenders.

- The Attackers should try to keep a tempo and move the ball constantly which in turn moves the Defenders around the rectangle, making it hard for them to win the ball.

- The Defenders should work as a foursome, pushing across where the ball is, blocking passing lanes, pressing the player in possession and making it hard to get passed through or around.

- Attackers should be playing the way they face and should be thinking ahead before they get the ball as to where they might pass it.

- Attackers on the sides should provide good angles when supporting the ball carrier.

☑ PROGRESSION:

- Instead of swapping every 3 times the Defenders win the ball, play for rounds of 5 minutes and Defenders ***don't*** swap when they win the ball. Instead the Defenders must keep possession in the rectangle for as long as they can. And the Attacker that gave away possession, plus their teammate to their left, must go into the rectangle to make it 3v4 and try and win back possession. Once they win back possession, reset and start again.

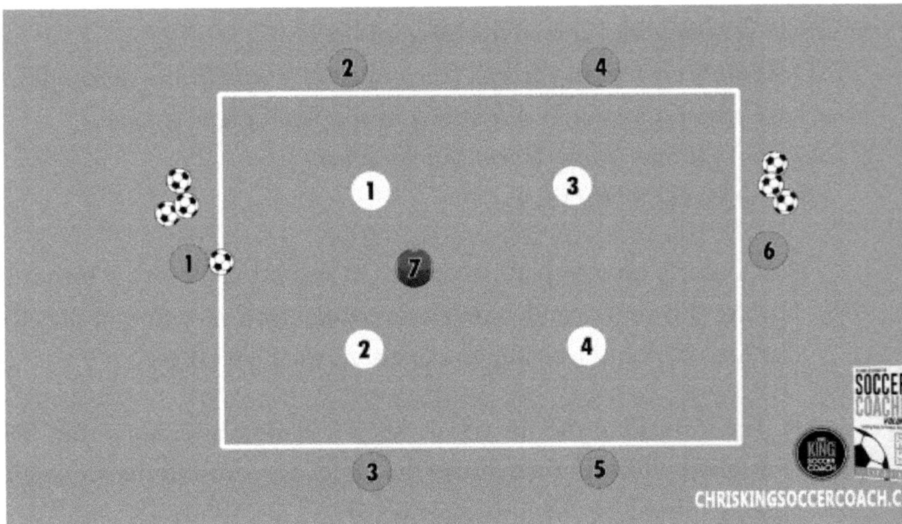

Similar to the rondo in the first drill, Reds/Dark must work the ball from end to end while using the centre player (Blue/Darker #7).

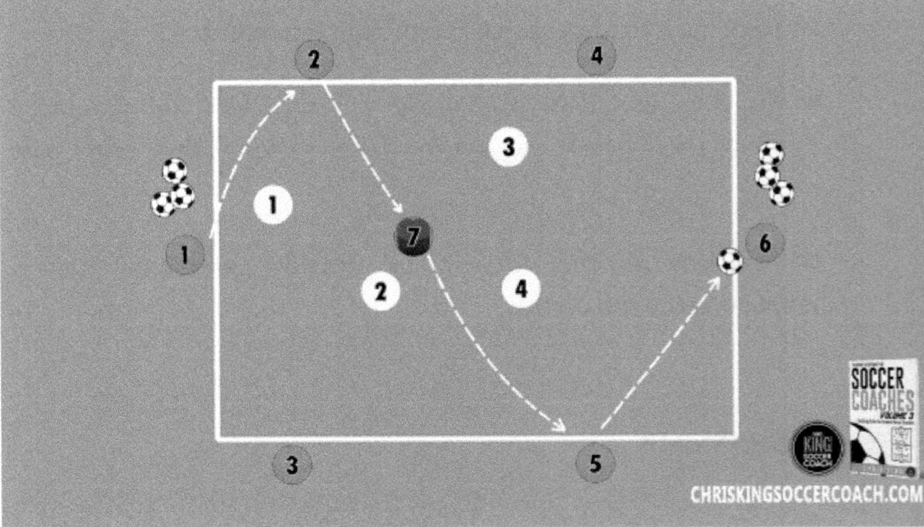

Yellow/Light haven't shut down passing lanes or marked the centre player tightly enough. Red/Dark is able to transition the ball to the other end (Defence to Attack!).

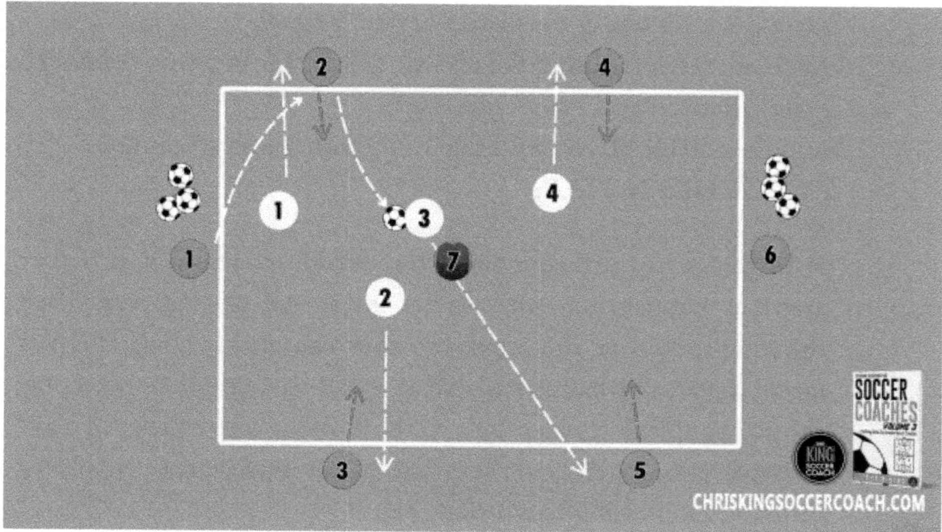

Yellow/Light #3 reads the play and intercepts the pass. The 4 Yellows have won possession 3 times so they swap with 4 Reds.

SESSION 9 "TRANSITION PLAY"
DRILL C (THE GAME PHASE)
"TRANSITION GAME "

◈ PURPOSE:

- A fast paced larger game to get players used to constantly transitioning from Attack to Defense.

◈ SET UP:

- **16 Players + 2 Goalkeepers**
- 40x35 yard rectangle
- 2 large goals

◈ THE DRILL:

4+4 v 4+4 plus goalkeepers.

4 from each team are spread around the outside of the playing area:

2 either side of the goal they are defending and the other 2 further up, 1 on each side closest to the goal they are attacking.

4 from each team start inside the rectangle (2-2 formation).

Play starts from one of the players beside the goal.

Quick, intense play using the outside players for one-twos where possible and getting shots on goal (shoot on sight!).

Swap the outside players with the inside players every 5 minutes.

◈ COACHES NOTES:

- In games like this sometimes the outside players feel as if they aren't as important as the players inside the playing area. Their thinking should be the opposite - they can greatly affect the play inside the area by being available as a wall pass option and keeping the play simple. It teaches them to think about where they can make a simple pass, whereas if they were in the middle they would be thinking about dribbling, turning etc.

- Goalkeepers will be peppered with shots from close range so it will help with their shot stopping.

- Can the team in possession keep a nice tempo of passing until an opportunity arises to get a shot on goal?

- Attackers should follow up shots for easy tap-ins (good habits such as this can add up to a few goals over a season).

☑ PROGRESSION:

- If a player passes to an outside player they swap roles. This helps teach players to move when they pass the ball.

- Make it one touch for the outside players and two touch maximum on the inside (or one touch for everyone).

- After a team wins the ball they must play to an outside player before being able to score.

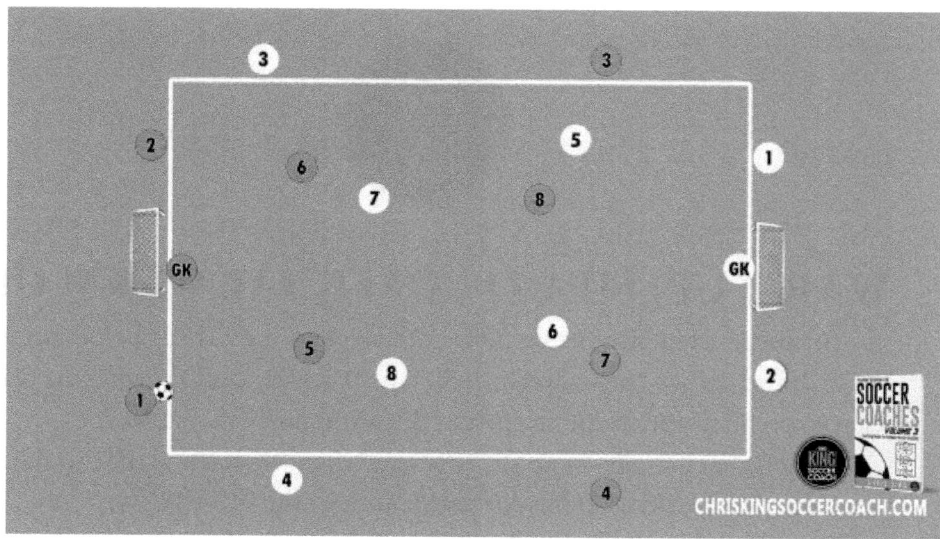

Starting line up of 4 players from each team spread around the outside and 4 players from each team inside the square. Play starts from a player beside their goal (in this case Red/Dark #1).

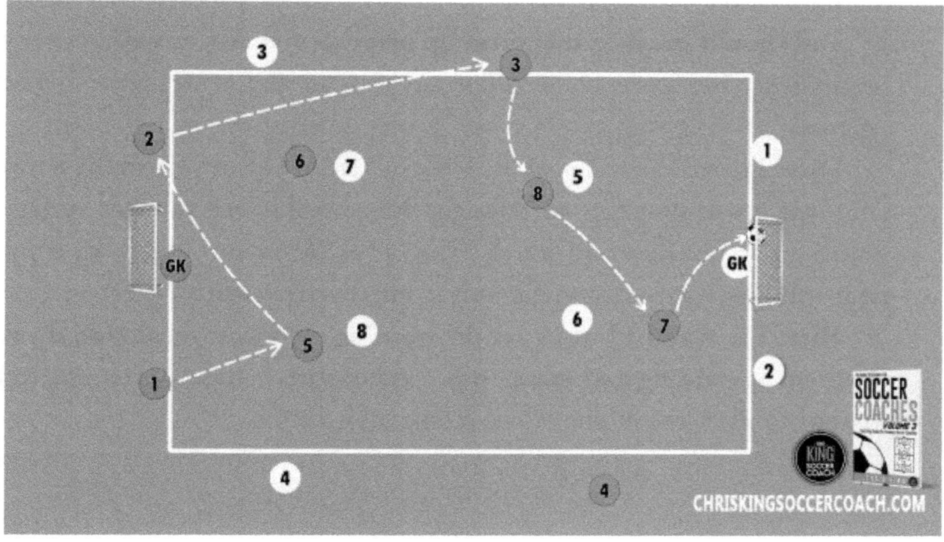

Reds/Dark pass the ball using the outside players to work the ball forward. Ending with getting the ball to Red/Dark #7 who finishes. Every 5 minutes swap the outside players with the inside players.

WARM UP: FIFA 11+ OFFICIAL WARM UP

For the last few seasons we have implemented the FIFA 11+[1] warm up at our club and we have benefited from it. After two weeks of showing the players what to do, they were running most of the warm up by themselves.

The coaches literally set up the cones and then when it was time to start the warm up, simply said "Get in your pairs and start the FIFA 11".

The FIFA 11+[2] warm up has been shown to reduce major injuries by 50% in recreational/grassroots football. It consists of three parts with a total of 15 exercises performed in order. It should be performed at the start of every training session.

You should use it as the warm up prior to matches as well but only the running exercises (parts 1 and 3), don't do the core and leg strengthening before a game!

I have inserted an image of the Official FIFA 11 Warm Up in the next page but if you are reading this on a device with a small screen you may struggle, so simply go on YouTube and search "The "11+" Warm-up: Part 1" or copy and paste this link[3]: https://www.youtube.com/watch?v=RSJIp7e7fyY

Parts 1 to 6 and 13 to 15 are the running exercises you should do as the warm up at training and match day. Add in parts 7 to 12 at training to help strengthen muscles but don't do this on match days.

---

1. https://www.youtube.com/watch?v=RSJIp7e7fyY
2. **https://www.youtube.com/watch?v=RSJIp7e7fyY**
3. https://www.youtube.com/watch?v=RSJIp7e7fyY

The FIFA 11+[4] program is broken down into 3 parts:

4. https://www.youtube.com/watch?v=RSJIp7e7fyY

1. Slow-speed running exercises coupled with active and partner stretching (8 minutes) - PARTS 1[5] T0 6 ON YouTube when you search ""The "11+" Warm-up: Part 1"

1. Core and leg strength exercises, along with balance, plyometrics, and agility exercises (12 minutes) - PARTS 7[6] T0 12 ON YouTube when you search ""The "11+" Warm-up: Part 1"

1. Moderate/high speed running exercises integrated with cutting and pivoting movements (2 minutes). - PARTS 13[7] T0 15 ON YouTube when you search ""The "11+" Warm-up: Part 1"

Setting it up: There are six pairs of parallel cones, approximately 5-6m apart. Two players start at the same time from the first pair of cones, jog along the inside of the cones and do the various exercises on the way at each set of cones.

After the last cone, they turn and run back along the outside. On the way back, speed can be increased progressively as players warm up.

The FIFA[8] 11+[9] is well worth implementing. Most of it can be done in a fairly small area and **the players look and feel more professional and therefore treat the rest of the session in a more professional manner.**

On the following page is a breakdown of the exercises that are performed in the first part. I would still suggest going to https://www.youtube.com/watch?v=RSJIp7e7fyY if you are unfamiliar with it as each exercise is shown in a video and explained.

---

5. https://www.youtube.com/watch?v=RSJIp7e7fyY
6. https://www.youtube.com/watch?v=gf-XEapqXPU&list=PLAPyvPaEZQXmX02V78z-je7e92iLfvD-G&index=7
7. https://www.youtube.com/watch?v=xTPjzXl_QIc&list=PLAPyvPaEZQXmX02V78z-je7e92iLfvD-G&index=25
8. https://www.youtube.com/watch?v=RSJIp7e7fyY
9. https://www.youtube.com/watch?v=RSJIp7e7fyY

The warm down after a training session or a game should be slow jogging and then walking with intermittent static stretches for approximately 10 minutes.

1. **Straight Ahead**[10]:[11] Jog straight to the last cone. Run slightly quicker on the way back. Do the exercise 2x.

1. **Running Hip Out:**[12] Jog to the first cone. Stop and lift your knee forwards. Rotate your knee to the side and put your foot down. Jog to the cone and do the exercise on the other leg. When you have finished the course, jog back. Do the exercise 2x.

1. **Running Hip In:**[13] Jog to the first cone. Stop and lift your knee to the side. Rotate your knee forwards and put your foot down. Jog to the next cone and do the exercise on the other leg. When you have finished the course, jog back. Do the exercise 2x.

1. **Circling Partner:**[14] Jog forward to the first cone. Shuffle sideways at a 90 degree angle towards your partner, shuffle an entire circle around one another (without changing the direction you are looking in) and back to the first cone. Jog to the next cone and repeat the exercise. When you have finished the course, jog back. Do the exercise 2x.

1. **Jumping with Shoulder Contact:**[15] Jog to the first cone. Shuffle sideways at a 90 degree angle towards your partner. In the middle, jump sideways towards each other to make shoulder-to-shoulder contact. Shuffle back to the first cone. Then jog to the next cone and repeat the exercise. When you have finished the course, jog back. Do the exercise 2x.

---

10. https://www.youtube.com/watch?v=RSJIp7e7fyY

11. https://www.youtube.com/watch?v=RSJIp7e7fyY

12. https://www.youtube.com/watch?v=rPugh9vf9Hg&t=2s

13. https://www.youtube.com/watch?v=dyeV-K5wmQA&t=1s

14. https://www.youtube.com/watch?v=67FEXBx_G6g&t=2s

15. https://www.youtube.com/watch?v=DlWuFO1e4Xc

1. **Quick Forwards and Backwards Sprints:**[16] Run quickly to the second cone then run backwards quickly to the first cone, keeping your hips and knees slightly bent. Repeat, running two cones forwards and one cone backwards. When you have finished the course, jog back. Do the exercise 2x.

You should try not to have long gaps between activities. When your warm up is complete, have a quick break for a drink, explain the first drill of the session and then start.

THANK YOU!

Thank you for purchasing my book, I hope you got some valuable information from it. I also have a Facebook page and website that I post new drills and information on regularly.

www.chriskingsoccercoach.com[17]

facebook.com/chriskingsoccercoach[18]

If you've enjoyed this book, please spend one minute giving the book a rating to help others find my book.

Till next time, thanks again and all the best with your coaching!

Chris King

Online Kids Coaching Course on Udemy.com:

https://www.udemy.com/course/

howtocoachkidssoccer/?referralCode=CCFEDDB18FE0AAF8F1CC

---

16. https://www.youtube.com/watch?v=-qLxW9S1CoM

17. http://www.chriskingsoccercoach.com

18. https://www.facebook.com/chriskingsoccercoach/

And if you need other coaching books have a look below.

I have full coaching sessions for senior players down to books for coaching kids which are perfect for parents or volunteers.

www.chriskingsoccercoach.com[19]

VIEW OTHER SOCCER COACHING BOOKS BY CHRIS KING

Training Sessions For Soccer Coaches Volume 1

Training Sessions For Soccer Coaches Volume 2

Training Sessions For Soccer Coaches Volume 3

Attacking & Shooting Drills For Soccer Coaches

Soccer Rondos Volume 1

Soccer Rondos Volume 2

Coaching Kids Soccer - Volume 1

Coaching Kids Soccer - Volume 2

Coaching Kids Soccer - Volume 3

The Ultimate Soccer Coaching Bundle Volume 1

110 Drills For Soccer Coaches

---

19. http://www.chriskingsoccercoach.com

TRAINING SESSIONS FOR
SOCCER
COACHES
VOLUME 1
Coaching Books For Amateur Soccer Coaches
CHRIS KING
TRAINING SESSIONS FOR
SOCCER
COACHES
VOLUME 2
Coaching Books For Amateur Soccer Coaches
CHRIS KING

TRAINING SESSIONS FOR
SOCCER
COACHES
VOLUME 3
Coaching Books For Amateur Soccer Coaches
CHRIS KING
TRAINING SESSIONS FOR
2 BOOKS IN 1
SOCCER
COACHES
VOLUMES 1+2
Coaching Books For Amateur Soccer Coaches
CHRIS KING

TRAINING SESSIONS FOR
SOCCER
COACHES
3 BOOKS IN 1!
VOLUMES 1,2,3
Coaching Books For Amateur Soccer Coaches
CHRIS KING
ATTACKING & SHOOTING DRILLS FOR
SOCCER
COACHES
VOLUME 1
Coaching Books For Amateur Soccer Coaches
CHRIS KING

SOCCER
RONDOS
VOLUME 1
Coaching Books For Amateur Soccer Coaches
CHRIS KING
SOCCER
RONDOS
VOLUME 2
Coaching Books For Amateur Soccer Coaches
CHRIS KING

2 BOOKS IN 1
SOCCER
RONDOS
VOLUMES 1+2
Coaching Books For Amateur Soccer Coaches
CHRIS KING

COACHING
KIDS SOCCER
AGES 5 TO 10
VOLUME 1
This book is for first time coaches, volunteers, parents and anyone wanting to coach!
Set up simple, fun and effective drills and organise a training session in 5 minutes!
CHRIS KING
COACHING
KIDS SOCCER
AGES 5 TO 10
VOLUME 2
This book is for first time coaches, grassroots coaches, volunteers and parents!
Set up simple soccer drills that teach kids skills while having fun!
CHRIS KING

COACHING
KIDS SOCCER
AGES 5 TO 10
VOLUME 3
This book is for first time coaches, volunteers & any would be coach
Set up simple, fun and effective drills & organise a practice session in 5 minutes!
CHRIS KING
2 BOOKS IN 1
COACHING
KIDS SOCCER
VOLUMES 1+2
This book is for first time coaches, volunteers & any would be coach
Set up simple, fun and effective drills & organise a practice session in 5 minutes!
CHRIS KING

COACHING
KIDS SOCCER
VOLUMES 1,2,3
This book is for first time coaches, grassroots coaches, volunteers and parents!
Set up simple soccer drills that teach kids skills while having fun! Includes 3 Volumes!
CHRIS KING

5 BOOKS IN 1!
THE ULTIMATE
SOCCER
COACHING
BUNDLE
VOLUME ONE
CHRIS KING
7 BOOKS IN 1!
110
DRILLS FOR
SOCCER
COACHES
Coaching Books For Amateur Soccer Coaches
THIS BOOK INCLUDES 7 BOOKS IN 1!
CHRIS KING

Don't miss out!

Visit the website below and you can sign up to receive emails whenever Chris King publishes a new book. There's no charge and no obligation.

https://books2read.com/r/B-A-QGPU-OTONC

BOOKS 2 READ

Connecting independent readers to independent writers.

Also by Chris King

Coaching Kids Soccer

Coaching Kids Soccer - Ages 5 to 10 - Volume 1

Coaching Kids Soccer - Ages 5 to 10 - Volume 2

Coaching Kids Soccer - Ages 5 to 10 - Volume 3

Coaching Kids Soccer - Volumes 1-2-3

Coaching Kids Soccer - Volumes 1 & 2

50 Tips On How To Coach A Children's Soccer Team

Kicking It With Santa: 20 Fun Christmas Themed Soccer Drills and Games (3 to 10 year olds)

The Beginner's Guide To Coaching Kids Soccer (Ages 5 to 10) - A Complete Resource For Parents And Volunteers - From First Practice To Game Day

Coaching Soccer

Training Sessions For Soccer Coaches - Volume 1

Soccer Rondos Volumes 1 and 2

Training Sessions For Soccer Coaches

Training Sessions For Soccer Coaches Volume 2

Training Sessions For Soccer Coaches Volume 3

The Ultimate Soccer Coaching Bundle (5 books in 1) Volume 1

Training Sessions For Soccer Coaches Volumes 1-2-3

Standalone

10 Soccer Drills -Volume 1

www.ingramcontent.com/pod-product-compliance
Ingram Content Group UK Ltd.
Pitfield, Milton Keynes, MK11 3LW, UK
UKHW021920190726
13853UKWH00002B/757

9 798223 278139